ENGLISH live

Ausgabe A
Band 1

D1735099

Laurence Harger · Malcolm Sexton · Terry Moston

Das Londoner Parlamentsgebäude mit Uhrturm, in dem die als „Big Ben" bekannte Glocke hängt.

Langenscheidt-Longman
ENGLISH LANGUAGE TEACHING

westermann®

English live
Ausgabe A, Band 1
für das 5. Schuljahr

Autoren:
Laurence Harger
Malcolm Sexton
Terry Moston

Mitarbeiter:
Waldemar Bindseil, Soltau
Prof. Dr. Wolf-Dietrich Bald, Universität Köln
Dr. Werner Kieweg, Universität München
Adolf Schwarz, Eichenau
Anne Wichmann-Jones, Lancaster University
Celine Sawicki, Münster

Beratende Mitwirkung:
Maria Kieweg, Schwabmünchen
Ursula Röttger, Senden
Prof. Peter Doyé, Technische Universität Braunschweig

Verlagsredaktion:
Stefanie Besser

Zeichnungen:
Peter Stevenson (Linden Artists)
Jörg Plannerer
David Vaughan

Graphik:
Beate Andler-Teufel
Sieglinde Milbradt (Typodata GmbH)

Umschlag:
Zero Grafik & Design GmbH

ENGLISH LIVE 1A umfasst folgende Lehrwerksteile:	
	Best.-Nr.
Schülerbuch	25 0600
Workbook & Activities	25 0606
Textcassette	25 7165
Lehrerhandreichungen	25 0612
Folien	25 7177
Lernkontrollen	25 0618
Lernkontrollen Testcassette	25 7171
Lernkontrollen LHR	25 0624

Der Innenteil dieses Buches wurde auf chlorfrei gebleichtem Papier gedruckt.

1. Auflage
© 1996 Langenscheidt-Longman GmbH, München und Westermann Schulbuchverlag GmbH, Braunschweig
© (Erstausgabe) 1990 Langenscheidt-Longman GmbH, München

Druck: westermann druck, Braunschweig
Printed in Germany
ISBN 3-14-25 0600-4

4 5 6 7 / 00 99 98 97

Hello!

Siehst du, liebe Schülerin, lieber Schüler, schon hast du das erste englische Wort gelesen!
Du kennst sicher die Hitparade, wo Singles und LP's vorgestellt werden. Hast du nicht auch schon Geschichten von Mickey Mouse gelesen? Nun, schon wieder einige englische Wörter!

Durch dein erstes Englischjahr begleiten dich Kim, Pat und Madur, Grant, Alec und John, aber auch der alte Seemann Len mit Skipper und seinem lustigen Affen Mr Christian. Deine englischen Freunde wohnen alle in oder bei Portsmouth. Suche es doch einmal auf der Karte *(Seite XII)*! Bestimmt ins Herz schließen wirst du auch den Clown Coco, einen fröhlichen Kerl, der immer für eine Überraschung gut ist – also vergiss ihn nicht!

Coco

Deine englischen Freunde findest du nicht nur im Buch, du kannst sie – sozusagen live – auch auf der Textcassette 📼 erleben. Sicher willst du im Englischunterricht auch mit deinen Mitschülern sprechen, immer voll in action sein. Dafür gibt es Partnerübungen 👥 und Gruppenübungen 👥👥. Häufig könnt ihr auch über euch selbst und eure eigenen Erlebnisse reden *(Now you.)*. Mit Kim, Alec, Len, Skipper und Coco, den Liedern, Reimen, Rätseln und Geschichten macht es dir bestimmt viel Spaß, Englisch zu lernen. Das wünschen wir dir jedenfalls!

Mr Christian

Skipper

Len

Mark

Pat

Alec

Madur

Kim

Grant

Rita

John

The Grove Club

Paulsgrove

Castle School

Portchester

Portchester Castle

Portsmouth

Mountbatten Centre

Weltsprache Englisch

Canada
(Kanada)

United States
of America
(Vereinigte Staaten
von Amerika)

British
Isles
(Britische
Inseln)

Pakistan
(Pakistan)

India
(Indien)

African
Countries
(Afrikanische
Länder)

Australia
(Australien)

New Zealand
(Neuseeland)

Ghost hunters

The class play: Ghost hunters
Zwei Journalisten kommen in das Willis Hall
Tourist Hotel, um Fotos des Gespenstes für die
Hotelbroschüre zu machen. Um Mitternacht
sieht alles zuerst gut aus - aber dann läuft etwas
schief.
Listening
Acting

Zusammenstellung der wichtigsten Wort- und Sachfelder.

Übersichtliche Zusammenstellung der Grammatik, die in diesem Buch durchgenommen wird.

Zusammenstellung der englischen Wörter und Wendungen in der Reihenfolge der Units.

Zusammenstellung der englischen Wörter und Wendungen in alphabetischer Reihenfolge.

ii Partnerübungen kannst du mit einem Mitschüler zusammen machen.

iii Gruppenübungen kannst du gemeinsam mit mehreren Klassenkameraden bearbeiten.

i̊ Kettenübungen werden von der ganzen Klasse gemeinsam gemacht. Du antwortest einem Klassenkameraden und stellst
selbst eine weitere Frage an einen anderen Mitschüler.

▄▄ Texte, Übungen und Songs mit diesem Symbol findest du (auch) auf der Textcassette.

◯ Die Übungen mit dieser Kennung sind etwas schwieriger und können gegebenenfalls weggelassen werden.

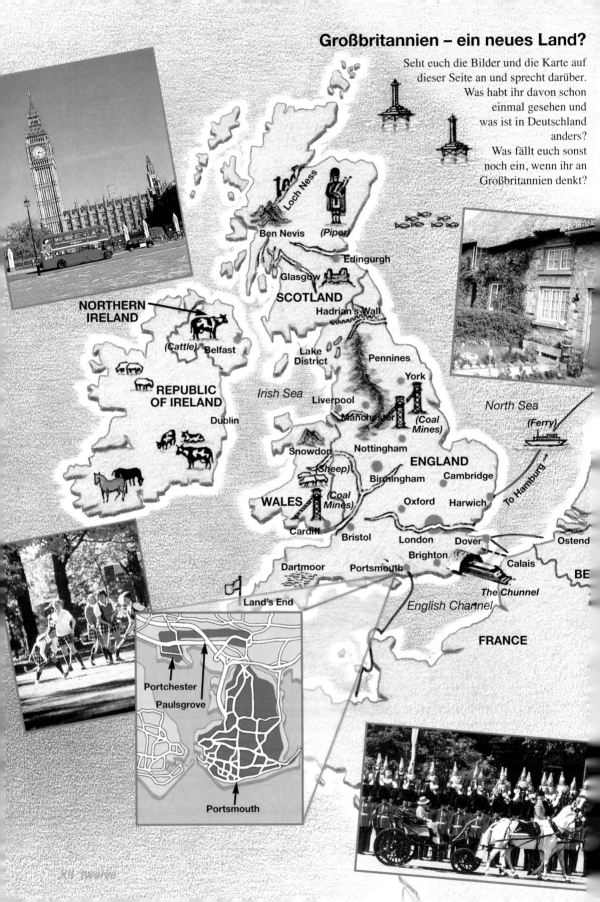

Großbritannien – ein neues Land?

Seht euch die Bilder und die Karte auf dieser Seite an und sprecht darüber. Was habt ihr davon schon einmal gesehen und was ist in Deutschland anders? Was fällt euch sonst noch ein, wenn ihr an Großbritannien denkt?

Loch Ness

Ben Nevis *(Piper)*

Edingurgh

Glasgow

SCOTLAND

Hadrian's Wall

NORTHERN IRELAND

(Cattle) Belfast

Lake District

Pennines

York

REPUBLIC OF IRELAND

Irish Sea

Liverpool

Manchester *(Coal Mines)*

North Sea

(Ferry)

Dublin

Snowdon

Nottingham

ENGLAND

(Sheep)

Birmingham

Cambridge

WALES *(Coal Mines)*

Oxford

Harwich

To Hamburg

Cardiff

Bristol

London

Dover

Ostend

Brighton

Calais

BE

Dartmoor

Portsmouth

The Chunnel

Land's End

English Channel

FRANCE

Portchester

Paulsgrove

Portsmouth

English words

Ihr kennt sicher schon eine Menge englischer Wörter!
Hier sind einige, die im Deutschen oft verwendet werden.

Für welche Wörter gibt es auch einen deutschen Begriff?

Jetzt übt mit eurem Lehrer/eurer Lehrerin, wie man diese Wörter so ausspricht, wie Engländer sie aussprechen würden. Kennt ihr weitere englische Wörter?

STEP 1

Hello!

Pat: Hello!
Alec: Hello. What's your name?
Pat: Pat. And what's your name?
Alec: I'm Alec.

Now you.

A: Hello!
B: Hello! What's your name?
A: I'm (Peter).
    And what's your name?
B: I'm (Silvia).

Good morning

Mr Wilson: Good morning.
               My name is George Wilson.
               What's your name?
Miss Green: I'm Miss Green. Jane Green.
Mr Wilson: Hello, Jane.

Mr Wilson: Are you Ann Dean?
Mrs Dean: Yes, I am.
Mr Wilson: Hello.

1 *Now you.*

A: Good morning. My name is (Peter).
B: Good morning. My name is (Silvia).
C: Good morning. My name is ...
D: ...

3 *Now you.*

A: Are you (Silvia)?
B: Yes, I am.
A: Hello, (Silvia).

2 *Now you.*

A: Good morning. My name is (Peter).
      What's ...?
B: I'm (Silvia).
A: Hello.

1 Jemanden begrüßen

Hello.	*Hallo.*
	Guten Tag.
Good morning.	*Guten Morgen.*

3 Das ist im Englischen anders:

You	=	**du** und **Sie**
Your (name)	=	**dein** (Name), **Ihr** (Name)

2 Fragen und sagen, wie jemand heißt

What's your name?	*Wie heißt du?*
	Wie heißen Sie?
I'm Silvia.	*Ich heiße Silvia.*
My name is Peter.	*Mein Name ist Peter.*
Are you Ann Dean?	*Bist du Ann Dean?*
	Sind Sie Ann Dean?

Are you English?

I'm Scottish.

I'm Italian.

I'm Greek.

I'm American.

I'm English.

I'm Turkish.

I'm German.

Alec:	Hello. I'm Alec.
Grant:	Oh. My name is Grant.
Alec:	Hello.
Grant:	Are you English?
Alec:	No, I'm not. I'm Scottish. And you? Are you English?
Grant:	Yes, I am.

1 *Ask and answer.*

1 *A:* Are you Turkish?
  B: No, I'm not.
  A: Are you English?
  B: Yes, I am.

2 *A:* Are you Greek?

3 *A:* Are you German?

4 *A:* Are you Italian?

5 *A:* Are you English?

6 *A:* Are you American?

7 *A:* Are you Scottish?

3 Let's say it.

[əʊ]
1 Hell**o**, **oh**, n**o**.
2 Hell**o**, are you Grant?
3 N**o**, I'm not.
4 **Oh**. I'm Alec.
5 Hell**o**.

2 *Now you.*

A: Are you (English)?
B: Yes, I am.
  No, I'm not. I 'm … And you?
A: I'm …

[dʒ]
1 **J**ane, **G**eor**g**e, **G**erman.
2 **J**ane and **G**eor**g**e.
3 **J**ane is English,
  Peter is **G**erman.

1 Fragen und sagen, welche Staatsangehörigkeit jemand hat

Are you English?	*Bist du Engländer(in)?*
	Sind Sie Engländer(in)?
I'm German.	*Ich bin Deutsche.*
	Ich bin Deutscher.

2 Das ist im Englischen anders:

name (**N**ame), **m**orning (**M**orgen)	Hauptwörter werden kleingeschrieben.
Yes, **I** am **G**erman.	Das Wort 'I' wird immer großgeschrieben.
	Die Staatsangehörigkeit wird auch großgeschrieben.

STEP 4

How are you?

Alec: Hello, Grant, how are you?
Grant: I'm fine, thanks.
         Alec, this is Rita, my sister.
         Rita, this is Alec.
Alec: Hello.
Rita: Hello.

1 Now you.

A: How are you?
B: I'm fine, thanks.
C: How are you?
D: I'm ...

2 What are they saying?

1   A: Rita, this is John.
          John, this is Rita.
     B: Hello.
     C: Hello.

2   ...

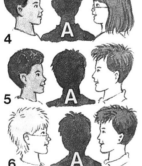

3 Now you.

A: (Silvia), this is (Peter).
     (Peter), this is (Silvia).
B: Hello.
C: Hello.

4 Now listen to the song
and sing it.

1 Fragen und sagen, wie es einem geht

How are you?   *Wie geht es dir?*
                      Wie geht es Ihnen?
I'm fine, thanks.   *Mir geht es gut, danke.*

2 Jemanden vorstellen

Alec, this is Rita.   *Alec, das ist Rita.*

• • • • • • **Good morning** • • • • • •

Good morn-ing, good morn-ing, good

morn-ing! And how are you this

morn-ing? Good morn-ing, good

morn-ing! And how are you to-

day____? I'm fine, thanks, I'm

fine, thanks, I'm fine, thanks, this

morn   -   ing. ____

Who's that?

Grant:	Who's that, Rita?
Rita:	Mr Wilson. He's nice.
Alec:	And who's that?
Rita:	That's Mrs Dean. She's the English teacher. She's okay.
Alec:	And who's that?
Rita:	That's Miss Green, the German teacher. She isn't nice. And German is awful.
Alec:	German isn't awful. German is nice.

1 ⁞⁞ *Ask and answer.*

A: Who's that?
B: That's ...

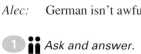

2 ⁞⁞ *Ask and answer.*
Look at the pictures in exercise 1.

A: Who's that?
B: That's ...

He's	nice.
She's	the German teacher.
	Scottish.
	okay.
	English.

3 *Test your teacher!*

Who's that?   That's (Silvia).   That's right!/ That's wrong!

Who's that?   I'm you!

4 *Talk about the people.*

He isn't ... He's ...
She isn't ... She's ...
He isn't English. He's Scottish.

1 Italian - Greek

2 German - Italian

3 English - German

4 American - English

5 Scottish - Turkish

6 Greek - Scottish

7 Turkish - American

5 *Talk about the people.*

Mr Wilson	is	okay.
Miss Green	isn't	nice.
Mrs Dean		

6 *Talk about the people.*

1 He's the English teacher.
2 She's the ... teacher.
3

7  Let's say it.

[ð]

1 **Th**is, **th**at, **the**.
2 Who's **th**at? Who's **th**is?
3 **Th**at's **the** English teacher.
4 And **th**at's **the** German teacher.

8 Words: please complete.

a - e - i - o - u

*ngl*sh　　m*rn*ng　　h*ll*　　t**ch*r
G*rm*n　*wf*l　　n*c*

---

1 Fragen und sagen, wer jemand ist

Who's that?　　　　*Wer ist das?*
That's Pat.　　　　*Das ist Pat.*

2 He isn't - she isn't

He isn't English.　　*Er ist kein Engländer.*
She isn't nice.　　　*Sie ist nicht nett.*

3 The

The wird normalerweise [ðə] ausgesprochen.
She's the [ðə] German teacher.
Vor **a e i o u** wird es [ðɪ] ausgesprochen.
He's the [ðɪ] **E**nglish teacher.

STEP 6

What's that in English?

Miss Green:	Good morning, boys and girls.
Boys & girls:	Good morning, Miss Green.
Miss Green:	Come in, please.
	Now, sit down, please.
	Now, listen, please.
Kim:	I'm Kim. What's your name?
Alec:	Alec.
Kim:	Hello.
Alec:	Hello.

Miss Green:	Now, what's 'Taschenrechner' in English? Kim.
Kim:	It's a calculator.
Miss Green:	Yes.
Alec:	What's that in German, please?
Miss Green:	Kugelschreiber.
Alec:	Klugelschreiber.
Miss Green:	No. Ku - gel - schrei - ber.
Alec:	Kugelschreiber.
Miss Green:	That's right.
	Now, stand up, please.

1 *What are they saying?*

Come in, please. - Sit down, please.
- Listen, please. - Stand up, please.

Come in, please.

2 *Now you.*

A: Stand up, please.
    Now, sit down, please.
B: Stand up, ...

4 *Ask and answer.*

A: What's that?   B: It's ...
    Who's that?

3 *Ask and answer.*

1 A: What's that in English, please?
   B: It's a book.
2 …

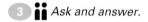

1 book
2 pen
3 rubber
4 chair
5 pencil
6 table
7 blackboard
8 window
9 biro
10 desk
11 school bag

5 *What are they saying?*

he - she - it

6 🔥 *Now you. Look at your classroom and ask your teacher.*

A: What's (Lichtschalter) in English, please?
T: It's …
B: What's …

1

Jim: Who's that?
Ann: That's Andy.
Jim: …'s okay.

2

Jim: Who's that?
Ann: That's Jane.
Jim: Oh, yes. …'s nice!

Jim: What's that?
Ann: …'s a chair.

3

1 Fragen und sagen, wie etwas auf Englisch heißt

What's that in English, please?	*Wie heißt das auf Englisch?*
What's 'Buch' in English, please?	*Wie heißt 'Buch' auf Englisch?*
It's a book.	*Es heißt 'book'.*

2 Das ist im Englischen besonders wichtig:

Bei Bitten sagt man so gut wie immer **'please'**.
'Thanks' musst du immer sagen, wenn jemand etwas für dich tut.

Vergiss die beiden Wörter nicht, sonst könnten Engländer oder Amerikaner denken, dass du unfreundlich bist.

That's my friend

Mark:	That's my classroom, mum.
Mrs Harman:	Is that your friend?
Mark:	No. That's my German teacher.
Mrs Harman:	She's a teacher! She's very small. What's her name?
Mark:	Miss Green.
Mark:	Look! That's my friend.
Mrs Harman:	What's his name?
Mark:	Grant.

1 👥 *Ask and answer.*

1 *A:* What's his name?
  B: His name is ...
2 ...

1 2 3 4

5 *A:* What's her name?
  B: ... name is ...
6 ...

5 6 7 8

2 *What are they saying?*

my - your - his - her

1

2

What's ... name?

That's ... pen!   3

Look! George and ... sister.

4

What's ... name?

5

That's ... desk!

6

Is that ... bag, Jane?

3 👬 *Ask and answer.*

A: What's (his/her) name?
B: ... name is ...

Henry   Alice   Jane   David   John   Mary

4 👬 *Now you. Test your partner.*

A: What's his name?
    What's her name?
B: That's (Peter).
A: That's right./That's wrong.

5 *What are they saying?*

I/my - he/his - she/her

I'm John and this is my team.

1 ...'m Grant and this is ...chair.
2 ...'m Mark and this is ...pen.
3 ...'s Andy and that's ... farm.
4 ...'s Mark and that's ... friend.
5 ...'s Kim and that's ... mum.
6 ...'s Jane and that's ... shop.

6 📼 *Let's say it.*

[æ]

1 Pat, Andy, that, thanks, and.
2 That's Pat, that's Andy.
3 Thanks, Pat.
4 Thanks, Andy.

7 *Words: make 2 lists.*

Italian – pen – rubber – Scottish – blackboard – English – German – book

Turkish	chair
Greek	pencil
...	...

1 Persönliche Fürwörter (Personal Pronouns)

I'm Grant.	*Ich heiße Grant.*
You're nice.	*Du bist nett.*
	Sie sind nett.
He's English.	*Er ist Engländer.*
She's okay.	*Sie ist okay.*
It's a rubber.	*Es ist ein Radiergummi.*

2 Besitzanzeigende Fürwörter (Possessive Pronouns)

I'm Pat.	This is **my** book.
You're okay.	That's **your** bag.
He's nice.	That's **his** pencil.
She's Italian.	This is **her** chair.

Sorry, dad!

Alec:	Oh, look, dad. That's Grant.
Mr Ross:	Is he your friend?
Alec:	Yes, he is.
	And that's Kim.
Alec:	Hello, Kim. Hello, Grant.
Kim &	
Grant:	Hello.
Grant:	Is that your house?
Alec:	Yes, it is.
Kim:	Is it nice?
Alec:	Yes, it is. It's big.
	That's my dad.
Kim:	What about your mum? Is she here?
Alec:	No, she isn't.
Alec:	Dad, this is Kim and this is Grant.
Mr Ross:	Hello.
	Oh no! Alec, you're awful!
Alec:	Sorry, dad.

1 👥 *Ask and answer.*

1 *A:* That's Kim.
    B: Is she nice?
    A: Yes, she is.

2 *A:* ... Grant.
    B: Is ... English?
    A: Yes, he ...

3 *A:* ... my house.
    B: Is ... nice?
    A: Yes, it ...

4 *A:* ... my pen.
    B: Is ... good?
    A: Yes, it ...

5 *A:* ... Mrs Dean.
    B: Is ... okay?
    A: Yes, she ...

6 *A:* ... Alec.
    B: Is ... Scottish?
    A: Yes, he ...

3 *Please answer.*

Yes, he   is.   No,   he   isn't.
        she   she
        it   it

Is she nice?
Yes, she is.

Is it big?

Is it small?

2 👥 *Ask and answer.*

1 *A:* Is he English?
    B: No, he isn't.

2 *A:* Is ... American?
    B: No, she ...

3 *A:* Is ... Italian?
    B: No, she ...

4 *A:* Is ... German?
    B: No, he ...

5 *A:* Is ... Turkish?
    B: No, he ...

6 *A:* Is ... Greek?
    B: No, he ...

7 *A:* Is ... Scottish?
    B: No, she ...

Is he awful?

Is she nice

Is it small?

4 *What are they saying?*

am - 'm - are - is - 's - isn't

Miss Green: ... you Alec Ross?
Alec: Yes, I ...
Miss Green: ... that your dad?
Alec: Yes, Miss.
Miss Green: ... you English?
Alec: No, I... not.
Miss Green: ... your dad English?
Alec: No, he ... He... Scottish.
Miss Green: And you? ... you Scottish?
Alec: Yes, I ...

5 ⏸ *Let's say it.*

[ɔ:]
1 Small, **aw**ful, m**or**ning, Ge**or**ge, y**our**.
2 A small **aw**ful boy.
3 Good m**or**ning, Ge**or**ge.
4 Oh, good m**or**ning. What's y**our** name?
5 I'm Ge**or**ge.

[ɜ:]
1 **Gir**l, **Ger**man.
2 **Ger**man **gir**l.
3 Sit down, **gir**ls.
4 Come in, **Ger**man **gir**ls.

We're Scottish

⏸

Mr Ross:	Hello. We're Mr and Mrs Ross.
Mr Smith:	Hello. My name is Orville Smith and this is Ruth.
Mrs Ross:	Hello. My name is Alison.
Mr Ross:	Yes, and I'm Stuart.
Mrs Smith:	Hello. Are you new here?
Mrs Ross:	Yes, we are. What about you?
Mrs Smith:	Oh, no, we aren't new here.
Mr Smith:	And are you English, Alison?
Mrs Ross:	No, we aren't. We're Scottish.
Mrs Smith:	Oh, you're Scottish? That's nice.
Mr Ross:	And what about you? Are you English?
Mrs Smith:	Yes, we are.

1 *What are they saying?*

I'm - We're

... German.

... American.

... Greek.

... English.

... Italian.

... Turkish.

2 ⫶⫶ *Ask and answer.*

1 Smith - Ross
    A: Are you Mr and Mrs Smith?
    B: No, we aren't. We're Mr and Mrs Ross.

2 Miller - Ross
3 Roberts - Miller
4 Wilson - Dean
5 Ross - Roberts
6 Miller - Wilson

4 ▭ *Let's say it.*

[aʊ]

1 About, down, house, how, now, sounds.
2 Sounds, sounds, sounds.
3 Sit down now.
4 Now, how are you?
5 This is my house. What about your house?

3 ⫶⫶ *Ask and answer.*

A: Are you (Turkish)?
B: Yes, we are.
    No, we aren't. We're ...

Persönliche Fürwörter (Personal Pronouns)

We're Mr and Mrs Ross.	*Wir sind Herr und Frau Ross.*
We aren't English.	*Wir sind keine Engländer.*
You're Scottish.	*Ihr seid Schotten.*
Are you Scottish?	Yes, **we are**.
Are you English?	No, **we aren't**.

They're new here

Mrs Smith:	Good morning, Stuart. Good morning, Alison.
Mr & Mrs Ross:	Hello, Ruth.
Mrs Smith:	That's Mr and Mrs Ross.
Ramesh Patel:	Mr and Mrs Ross? Are they new here?
Mrs Smith:	Yes, they are. They're Scottish.
Ramesh Patel:	Oh, they aren't English. They're Scottish.
	That's nice.

1 *Talk about the people.*

1 They're Scottish.
2 ...

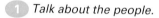

2 *Ask and answer.*

A: Are they ...?
B: Yes, they are.
   No, they aren't. They're ...

1 Mr and Mrs Smith - Scottish
   A: Are they Scottish?
   B: No, they aren't. They're English.

2 Grant and Rita - Scottish
3 Pat and John - English
4 Mr and Mrs Ross - English
5 Alec and Mr Ross - Scottish
6 Mark and Mrs Harman - American

3 *Let's say it.*

[u:]

1 Classr**oo**m, wh**o**, y**ou**.
2 Wh**o**'s that? That's y**ou**.
3 That's y**ou** and that's your classr**oo**m.
4 Wh**o**'s that? - That's y**ou**. - Wh**o**? - **You**.

4 *Words: Was sagst du, wenn ...*

1 du dich entschuldigen willst?
2 du dich bedanken willst?
3 du um etwas bittest?
4 du fragen willst, wie es jemandem geht?
5 du antworten willst, dass es dir gut geht?
6 du wissen willst, wie etwas auf Englisch
   heißt?

a) Sorry.
b) What's that in English?
c) Thanks.
d) Please.
e) How are you?
f) Fine, thanks.

5 *Classroom talk: what are they saying?*

1. Come in, please.
2. Sit down, please. / Thanks.
3. What's that in English?

1 Persönliche Fürwörter (Personal Pronouns)

They're Scottish.	*Sie sind Schotten.*
They aren't English.	*Sie sind keine Engländer.*

Are they new here?   Yes, **they are.**/No, **they aren't.**

2 Kurzformen (Short Forms)

Im Englischen werden **am are is** sehr häufig abgekürzt, besonders beim Sprechen.

Auch die Verneinung kannst du abkürzen.

Kurzform	Langform	Kurzform	Langform
I'm	I am	**I'm not**	I am not
we're	we are	**we aren't**	we are not
you're	you are	**you aren't**	you are not
they're	they are	**they aren't**	they are not
he's	he is	**he isn't**	he is not
she's	she is	**she isn't**	she is not
it's	it is	**it isn't**	it is not
who's	who is		
what's	what is		

Bei **Fragen und Antworten mit 'Yes/No'** benutzt man Kurzformen nur in der Antwort mit 'No':

Frage	Antwort mit Yes	Antwort mit No
Langform	**Langform**	**Kurzform**
Are you English?	**Yes, I am.**	**No, I'm not.**
Are you English?	**Yes, we are.**	**No, we aren't.**
Are we English?	**Yes, you are.**	**No, you aren't.**
Are they English?	**Yes, they are.**	**No, they aren't.**
Is he English?	**Yes, he is.**	**No, he isn't.**
Is she English?	**Yes, she is.**	**No, she isn't.**
Is it new?	**Yes, it is.**	**No, it isn't.**

1 📼 A quiz

1 Listen to the cassette.

2 Right or wrong?

a) Coco is a professor.
b) It's a German quiz.
c) Coco is English.
d) Professor is a name.
e) The question is: What's that in German?
f) 'Chair' is right.
g) 'Hellophone' is right.
h) 'Telephone' is wrong.

2 👥 Act the scene

A: Begrüße B.

B: Begrüße A.
      Frage A, wie er/sie heißt.

A: Sage, wie du heißt.
      Frage B, wie er/sie heißt.

B: Sage, wie du heißt.
      Frage A, ob er/sie Engländer/in ist.

A: Sage, du bist kein/e Engländer/in.
      Sage, aus welchem Land du kommst.

B: Frage, wer das (das andere Mädchen) ist.

A: Sage, sie ist deine Freundin.

B: Sage, sie ist nett.

A: Stimme zu.

B: Frage, wie sie heißt.

A: Sage, wie sie heißt.

Portsmouth is a big British port.

The "Victory"

This is Portsmouth

Paulsgrove is a new part
of Portsmouth.

**This is Portchester.
Portchester is an old town. It's near Portsmouth.**

This is a house
in West Street.

This is Castle Street in Portchester.

Portchester Castle

What's right?

Portsmouth	is	a	town near Portsmouth.
Paulsgrove		an	street in Portchester.
Portchester			big British port.
Castle Street			new part of Portsmouth.
West Street			old town.

Bighead!

Part 1

John:	Hello. Is Mark at home, please? We're his friends.
Mrs Harman:	Yes. Come in. He's in his room.

Part 2

Mark:	Hello. Look, I've got a computer. It's new.
Grant:	Wow! A computer!
John:	Very nice.
Mark:	Have you got a computer, John?
John:	Yes, I have.
Mark:	What about you, Grant? Have you got a computer?
Grant:	No, I haven't.
Mark:	I've got eight computer games. They're very good. This is a great game. Look.

Part 3

Mark:	Look. This is our television. And we've got a great stereo. Have you got a stereo?
John:	No, we haven't.
Mark:	We've got a hundred video cassettes! Have you got a car?
John:	Yes, we have. Our car is German.
Mark:	We've got two cars.

→ **A1**

→ **A2**

Part 4

John & Grant:	Goodbye, Mrs Harman.
Mrs Harman:	Goodbye, boys.

John:	Mark is a bighead! "I've got a computer and eight computer games."
Grant:	"This is our television. We've got two cars." What a bighead!
John:	Mark Bighead.

→ **A3**

A1 *What's missing?*

Mark: I've got a ...
 I've got eight ...
John: I've got ...

A2 *What's missing?*

Mark: We've got ... and we've got a hundred ...
 We've got two ...

A3 *What's right?*

John & Grant: 1 Mark is nice.
 2 Mark is big.
 3 Mark is a bighead.

A4 *Can you say the numbers?*

Numbers I

1 one	5 five	9 nine
2 two	6 six	10 ten
3 three	7 seven	11 eleven
4 four	8 eight	12 twelve

B

B1 *What's right?*

That's a/an ... car.
1 That's a British car.
2

B2 *What are they saying?*

1 I've got ...
2 ...

B3 👥 *Now you.*

A: I've got a (computer).
B: I've got a ...
C: ...

B4 *What are they saying?*

Jane: Have you got a ... in your room?
George: Yes, I have./No, I haven't.

B5 👥 *Now you.*

A: Have you got a ... in your room?
B: Yes, I have./No, I haven't.
 What about you?
A: Yes, .../No, ...

chair   bag   pen   pencil
window   desk   book   table ...
computer

B6 *What are they saying?*

1 We've got a house.
2 ...

She's nice.

B7 *Now you. Talk about your family.*

A: Have you got (a car)?
B: Yes, we have./No, we haven't.
 What about you?
A: Yes, ... /No, ...

television stereo
  computer ...

B8 *Now you. Talk about your family.*

A: Have you got (a stereo)?

B: Yes, our ... is   new.
    old.
    big.
    small.
    nice.
    okay.
    awful.

B9 *What are they saying?*

big - great - nice - small - awful

What a ... book!

... house!

What ... game!

... an ... chair!

... teacher!

B10 *Now you. Say the telephone numbers.*

one three five seven nine
two four six eight
five four three two one

A: What's your telephone number?
B: It's ... What's your telephone number?
C: It's ...

B11 *Words: what are they?*

a-e-i-o-u

1 Miss Green is the German t ** ch * r.
2 Grant and John are fr ** nds.
3 Grant and John are b * ys,
 Kim and Pat are g * rls.
4 Grant and John are * ngl * sh.
 What ab ** t you?
5 We've got a G * rm * n car.

B12 *Words: two together.*

1 **big**	5 new
2 goodbye	6 please
3 hello	7 old
4 **small**	8 thanks

B13 Let's say it.

[s]

1 Ca**ss**ettes, book**s**, desk**s**.
2 Ca**ss**ettes and book**s**.
3 Book**s** and desk**s**.
4 Desk**s** and book**s**.
5 Desk**s**, book**s**, ca**ss**ettes.

[tʃ]

1 **Ch**air, Por**tch**ester, tea**ch**er.
2 He's a tea**ch**er in Por**tch**ester.
3 That's your **ch**air, tea**ch**er.
4 One tea**ch**er, two tea**ch**ers, three tea**ch**ers.

[z]

1 Friend**s**, game**s**, car**s**, boy**s**, girl**s**.
2 Friend**s** and game**s**.
3 Friend**s** and car**s**.
4 Boy**s** and girl**s**.
5 Girl**s** and boy**s**.
6 Girl**s**, boy**s**, car**s**, game**s**, friend**s**.

[aɪ]

1 B**i**ro, f**i**ne, f**i**ve, **I**'ve, n**i**ce, n**i**ne.
2 Four and f**i**ve is n**i**ne.
3 **I**'ve got f**i**ve n**i**ce b**i**ros.
4 K**i**m is n**i**ce. **I**'m f**i**ne.

C

1 A - an

I've got **a** new stereo.
Mark is **a** boy.

I've got **an** old stereo.
Mark is **an** English boy.

Vor **a - e - i - o - u** wird **a** zu **an**.

2 The

the = der, die, das

The boy is nice.
The town is old.
The car is big.

Der Junge ist nett.
Die Stadt ist alt.
Das Auto ist groß.

3 Sagen und fragen, was jemand besitzt: have got

I've got a television.
(I have got)
We've got two cars.
(We have got)
Have you got a stereo?

Ich habe einen Fernseher.

Wir haben zwei Autos.

Hast du eine Stereoanlage?
Habt ihr eine Stereoanlage?

Yes, **I have.**
Yes, **we have.**

No, **I haven't.**
No, **we haven't.**

D1 **Classroom talk**

Please read.

Say that again, please.

It's your turn.

Say it in English, please.

D2 **A rhyme**

Say the rhyme.

One, two, three, four,
Come in, please, and close the door.
Five, six, seven, eight,
What's your name? You're very late.
Nine, ten, nine, ten,
Sorry, teacher, late again.

D3

Ask and answer.

Mark	**John**	**Grant**	**Rita**	**Kim**	**Coco**
car	car	book	stereo	computer	stereo
television	book	chair	pen	television	desk
chair	table	school bag	television	school bag	television
pen	house	stereo	biro	biro	biro
stereo	television	pen	desk	desk	telephone

A: Have you got ...?
Have you got ...?
...

B: Yes, I have.
No, I haven't.

A: You're (Grant).

B: That's wrong!

A: You're (Kim).

B: That's right!

1 What's right?

a - an

XXX: "My house is in Portchester. It's ... new house. Portchester is near Portsmouth. It's ... old town. I've got ... English stereo and ... American computer. My school is in Paulsgrove. Paulsgrove is ... new part of Portsmouth. We've got ... Scottish boy in our class."

Who is XXX ? Kim?
John?
...

2 What are they saying?

I - you - he - she - they

1 *Bill:* That's Jim. ...'s very nice.
2 *Stuart:* ...'m Stuart. Hello.
3 *Stuart:* Are ... Orville?
   Orville: Yes, ... am.
4 *Grant:* This is Rita. ...'s my sister.
5 *Ruth:* That's Mr and Mrs Ross. ...'re new here.

3 What are they saying?

my - your - his - her - our

1 *John:* That's ... dad.
   Grant: What's ... name?
   John: Bill. What about ... dad? What's ... name?
   Grant: ... name is Orville.

2 *Mark:* Who's that?
   Kim: She's ... friend.
   Mark: What's ... name?
   Kim: Pat.

3 *Grant:* Is that ... pen, Mark?
   Mark: No, it isn't. This is ... pen.

4 *Alec:* This is ... friend. ... name is Kim.

5 *Kim & Pat:* We're good friends. Miss Green is ... teacher.

6 *Mr & Mrs Smith:* ... name is Smith.

4 What are they saying?

this - that

1 *Miss Green:* ... is Alec Ross. He's Scottish.

2 *Mrs Harman:* Who's ...?
   Mark: ...'s our new teacher.

3 *Kim:* Alec, ... is Grant and ... is John. John, Grant, ... is Alec.

4 *Miss Green:* ... is your desk, Grant, and ...'s your desk, Alec.

5 *What's that in English?*

1 Wer ist das?
2 Sehr schön!
3 Uns geht's gut, danke.
4 Wiederhole das, bitte.
5 Wie heißt du?
6 Guten Morgen.

a) What's your name?
b) Say that again, please.
c) Good morning.
d) Who's that?
e) Very nice.
f) We're fine, thanks.

6 *Words: what are they?*

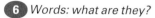

sport — it — hop — ay — treet — ong — he — mall

7 *Write about your family.*

Hello.
My name is Grant.
I'm English.

My house is in Paulsgrove. Paulsgrove is a new part of Portsmouth.
Our house is okay. Our telephone number is 63124.

This is my father. His name is Orville.
This is my mother. Her name is Ruth.

This is Rita. She's my sister. She's awful.

This is my room. In my room I've got a chair, a desk and an old stereo.

Now you.

1 Take a piece of paper.
2 Stick photos of your family on it: your mother, your father, your brother, sister, cousin, aunt and uncle.

3 Stick photos of your house and room on it, too.
4 Now write about the photos.

A problem

1 John and Grant are on their bikes.

2 They've got a problem.
They haven't got a pump.

A

Len Bignall

Part 1

Len:	Hey, you've got a flat tyre!
Grant:	Yes, and we haven't got a pump.
Len:	My name is Len Bignall.
Boys:	Hello, Mr Bignall.
Len:	Not Mr Bignall. I'm Len. What are your names?
Grant:	I'm Grant and this is John.

Part 2

Len: Grant has got a problem.
He hasn't got a pump, Skipper.

This is Skipper. She's got a pump.
Now, Skipper, get the pump, good dog!

Come in, boys.

→

Part 3

Grant:	You've got a monkey, too! What's his name, Len?
Len:	This is Mr Christian.
John:	Len, how old is Mr Christian?
Len:	He's an old monkey. He's ten.
John:	How old is Skipper?
Len:	She's eight. How old are you?
John:	I'm eleven. Grant is twelve.

→ **A2** **A3**

Part 4

Len:	Is it teatime, Mr Christian? Tea, boys?
John:	Yes, please, Len.
Len:	The cups are in the cupboard.
Grant:	Oh, yes. How many, Len? Three?
Mr Christian:	Eeek!
Grant:	Sorry, Mr Christian. Is this your cup?

John:	The milk and sugar are on the table.
Grant:	Okay, now it's teatime.
Len:	Good.
John:	Len is nice.
Grant:	Yes, and his pets are clever.

→ **A4** **A5**

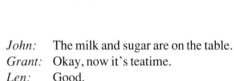

A1 *What's right?*

Len	has got	a pump.
Skipper	hasn't got	a flat tyre.
Grant		a problem.
John		

A2 *What's right?*

Len Bignall	is	a dog.
Mr Christian		a monkey.
Skipper		an old man.

A3 *Please answer.*

1 How old is John?
2 What is Mr Christian?
3 How old is he?
4 What is Skipper?

A4 *What's right?*

Len	has got	the cups.
Mr Christian		the milk and sugar.
Grant		his cup.
John		the tea.

A5 *What's right?*

| The milk | is | in the cupboard. |
| The sugar | isn't | on the table. |

B

B1 *Talk about the people.*

they're - their

1 They're old. This is their house.
2 ... German. This is ... farm.
3 ... professors. This is ... book.
4 ... American. This is ... car.
5 ... nice. This is ... shop.

B2 *Talk about the people.*

A: Number one is Anne. She's got a desk.
B: Number two is Jim. He's got ...
C: ...

1 Anne
2 Jim
3 George
4 Jane
5 Mike
6 Susan

B3 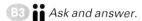 _Ask and answer._

A: Has (Mark) got a ...?
B: Yes, he has./No, he hasn't.

A: Has Mrs Harman got ...?
B: Yes, she has./No, she hasn't.

	Mark	Mr Harman	Mrs Harman
computer	*		
television		*	*
car		*	*
desk	*		
stereo		*	*
bike	*		
house		*	*
handbag			*
shop		*	

B4  _Now you._

A: I haven't got ...!
B: ...

book   computer   house   pen
car   dog   television   stereo   desk   bike ...

B5 _What's right?_

1 (Grant) hasn't got a ..
2 ...

	Grant	Mark	Mr Christian	Len	John
computer		*			*
television				*	*
stereo	*				
pump		*		*	
cup	*		*		

B6 _Now you. Ask about the people in your class._

A: Has (Silvia) got a ...?
B: Yes, she has./No, she hasn't.

C: Has (Peter) got ...?
D: Yes, he has./No, he hasn't.
E: ...

computer   telephone   sister
bike   dog   calculator ...

B7 *What are they saying?*

have - has

1 *Grant:* Mark ... got a computer. ... you got
      one, Kim?
  Kim: Yes, I ...
  Grant: Mark ... got eight computer games,
      too.
  Kim: ... he got a television, too?
  Grant: Yes, he ...

2 *John:* Len ... got two pets.
  Pat: Two pets? What are they?
  John: Len ... got a monkey and a dog.
  Pat: A monkey! Great! ... you got a pet,
      John?
  John: Yes, we ... We've got a dog, too.

B8 *Ask and answer.*

1 *A:* How old is Grant? *B:* He's twelve.
2 *A:* ... John? *B:* ...
3 *A:* ... Skipper? *B:* ...
4 *A:* ... Mr Christian? *B:* ...

B9 *Now you.*

A: How old are you?
B: I'm ... How old are you?
C: ...

B10 *Ask and answer.*

A: How many (books) has (Kim) got?
B: (She's) got (twelve books) and (a bike), too.

	Kim	Len	Grant	Pat	John	Ann
book	12					
cassette					11	
pen			8	6		7
bike	1					
desk				2		
chair		5	4		3	
cup		9				10

B11 *English words?*

1 neykom   4 limk
2 emattie   5 argus
3 bodarpuc   6 eta

B12 *What are they saying?*

at - in - on

1 Hello. I'm Grant. - Oh, yes. Come ...
2 John is not ... home.
3 We've got tea and sugar ... the cupboard.
4 The boys are ... their bikes.

B13 *Let's say it.*

[ʌ]
1 Cup, cupboard, pump, rubber.
2 One, come, number, monkey.
3 Cups in the cupboard.
4 Pumps in the cupboard.
5 Come in, number one.
6 Number one, monkey, come.

[v]
1 Clever, have, seven, eleven, Paulsgrove,
  television, very, video.
2 I'm clever, you're very clever.
3 We've got eleven televisions.
4 Oh, I've got seven clever videos.
5 Paulsgrove video club.

[iː]
1 Monkey, please, Rita, scene, street,
  tea, three.
2 Act the scene, please, teacher.
3 Rita and Peter and Peter and Rita.
4 A monkey in the street.

Riddle

What is it?

A giraffe passing a window.

1 How old?

How old are you, John?
I'm eleven.
How old is Skipper, Len?
She's eight.

Wie alt bist du, John?
Ich bin elf.
Wie alt ist Skipper, Len?
Sie ist acht.

2 How many?

How many cups, John?
Three.
How many games have you got, Mark?
I've got eight games.

Wie viele Tassen, John?
Drei.
Wie viele Spiele hast du, Mark?
Ich habe acht Spiele.

3 Sagen und fragen, was jemand besitzt: have got

I've got   a house.
(I have got)
You've got
(You have got)
We've got
(We have got)
They've got
(They have got)

He's got   a house.
(He has got)
She's got
(She has got)
It's got
(It has got)

I haven't got   a house.
(I have not got)
You haven't got
(You have not got)
We haven't got
(We have not got)
They haven't got
(They have not got)

He hasn't got   a house.
(He has not got)
She hasn't got
(She has not got)
It hasn't got
(It has not got)

Have you got a house?

Yes, **I have.** / No, **I haven't.**
Yes, **we have.** / No, **we haven't.**

Have they got a dog?

Yes, **they have.** / No, **they haven't.**

Has he got a friend?
Has she got a bike?

Yes, **he has.** / No, **he hasn't.**
Yes, **she has.** / No, **she hasn't.**

4 Besitzanzeigende Fürwörter (Possessive Pronouns)

I haven't got a new pen.
How are **you**?
He's got a problem.
She hasn't got a problem.
We are clever.
They are here.

My pen is old.
Is this **your** friend?
His tyre is flat.
It's **her** pump.
This is **our** new computer.
This is **their** dog.

D

D1 ▄ Len at home

1 What's right?

Number one is   a concertina.
…   a fisherman.
                a ship in a bottle.
                a tin.
                a worm.

3 Now listen again.

a) How many cups have they got?
b) How many worms has Len got?
c) How many ships in bottles has Len got?

4 Now listen to the song and sing it.

What shall we do with the drunken sailor

What shall we do with the drunken sailor,
What shall we do with the drunken sailor,
What shall we do with the drunken sailor,
Early in the morning?

     Hooray and up she rises,
     Hooray and up she rises,
     Hooray and up she rises,
     Early in the morning.

Put him in the long boat till he's sober,
Put him in the long boat till he's sober,
Put him in the long boat till he's sober,
Early in the morning.

     Hooray …

(Traditional song)

2 Now listen to the cassette.

Has Len got   worms in a tin?
               sweets?
               a concertina?

drunken = *betrunken*   long boat = *Beiboot*
hooray = *Hurra*   sober = *nüchtern*

D2 Paulsgrove club magazine

Read the article.

Our friend Len

We've got a new friend. His name is Len. He's not in our class.
His house is in Castle Street. That's in Portchester, not Paulsgrove. It's a very old house and Len is a very old man. Len has
got two pets - a dog and a monkey! Skipper is his dog. The
monkey is Mr Christian. Mr Christian is ten. Len has got great
things in his house. He's got a concertina and six ships in
bottles. And he's got worms in a tin - he's a fisherman. Len is
an old fisherman. He's very old but very nice. And he's our new
friend. Our new friend, Old Len.

John Roberts and Grant Smith

D3 A friend

Look at the article (D2) and write about a friend.
Here's some help.

What's his/her name?
How old is he/she?
What things has he/she got? - Pets, stereo, ...

1 What's in the picture? Write the words.

2 ⅱ *Play the game.*

Have you got a ... in your pocket?

Yes, I have./No, I haven't.

3 ⅱ *What's the difference?*

Hier und auf Seite 116 findet ihr zwei sehr ähnliche Bilder. Sie enthalten jedoch acht kleine Unterschiede, die ihr in Partnerarbeit herausfinden könnt. Einer von euch sieht das Bild auf dieser Seite an, der andere schlägt die Seite 116 auf. Fragt eueren Partner nach seinem Bild!

Have you got ...?   Is ... in/on ...?

Has ... got ...?   I've got ... in my picture. What about you?

What's the time?

1

7:30

Half past seven/Seven thirty

2

8:00

Eight o'clock

3

9:00

Nine o'clock

What's the time, please?

1 It's half past seven.
2 It's ...

4

4:00

Four o'clock

5

5:30

Half past five/Five thirty

A

Five o'clock in Paulsgrove

Part 1

Kim:	Hello, Ramesh.
Ramesh:	Hello, Kim. Hello, John.
John:	Where's Madur? Is she at home?
Ramesh:	No, she isn't.

Kim:	What's she doing?
Ramesh:	She's shopping.
John:	Oh!
Ramesh:	She's buying vegetables.

→ **A1**

Part 2

John:	Look! Madur. What's she doing? Is she talking to the flowers?
Kim:	Yes, she is. Oh, no, she isn't. She's washing her vegetables.
John:	Hey, Madur! What are you doing?
Madur:	I'm helping this bird.
Kim:	Oh, it's ill.
John:	Let's take it to Len's house. He's got a dog and a monkey. And he's very nice.
Madur:	Okay. Let's go.

→ **A2**

Part 3

Woman:	Are you helping that bird?
Madur:	Yes, I am. It's ill.

Man:	Are you playing with that bird?
Madur:	No, I'm not. I'm helping it.
John:	She's taking it to my friend Len.
Man:	Oh, that's all right.

→ A3

Part 4

John:	Len, this is Madur and this is Kim. We've got a bird. It's ill. Please take it.
Len:	Oh dear, I've got Skipper already.
Mr Christian:	Eeek!
Len:	Yes, yes. And I've got you!
Madur:	Please, Len.
Len:	Oh, all right.
Madur:	Thank you, Len.
Len:	Help me, please. Let's put it in the basket. Mr Christian, you've got a new friend. His name is ... er ... Sam.

→ A4 A5

A1 *What's right?*

Madur   is   at home.
          isn't   buying vegetables.
                  shopping.

A2 *What's right?*

Madur   is   talking to   a bird.
          isn't washing   her vegetables.
                 helping   the flowers.

A3 *What's right?*

Madur   is   playing with   the bird.
                 helping

A4 *What are they saying?*

1 *John:* We've got ...
2 *Len:* I've got ...
3 *Len:* You've got ...

A5 *Please answer.*

1 Has Mr Christian got a new friend?
2 What's his name?

B

B1 ⚎ *Ask and answer.*

1 A: What's the time, please?
   B: It's half past five.
2 A: What's ...?
   B: It's two o'clock.
3 A: ...?
   B: ...

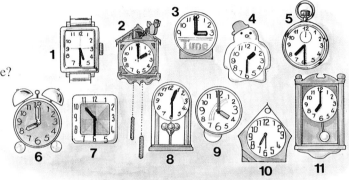

B2 *Write the time.*

1 It's 6.30.
2 ...

1 Half past six	5 Five o'clock
2 Eight o'clock	6 Half past three
3 Nine o'clock	7 Half past four
4 Half past two	8 One o'clock

B3 ⚎ *Ask and answer.*

go - help - play - shop - buy

1 A: What's Ann doing?
   B: She's shopping.
2 A: What's ...?
   B: He's ... his mother.
3 A: ...?
   B: He's ... flowers.
4 A: ...?
   B: She's ... with her computer.
5 A: ...?
   B: He's ... to Jane's house.

B4 ⚎ *Ask and answer.*

A: Where's the (monkey)?
B: He's (on) ...
    She's (in) ...

B5 Ask and answer.

A: Where are the monkey and the bird?
B: They are on/in ...

B6 Now you. Play the game.

1 *A* lässt seine Schulsachen im Klassenzimmer und geht hinaus.
2 Die anderen verstecken seine Bücher, Stifte etc. in oder auf dem Tisch.
3 *A* kommt zurück und fragt nach seinen Sachen:

A: Where's my (pen)?
   Is it in/on ...?
B: Yes, it is.
C: No, it isn't.
D: cold - warm - hot
E: ...

B7 What are they saying?

buy - go - help - wash

B8 What's right?

1 That's Mr Harman's house.
2 That's ...

B9 *Now you. Play the game.*

1   A verlässt das Klassenzimmer.
2   Die Schulsachen von verschiedenen Mit-
     schülern werden auf ein Pult gelegt.
3   A kommt zurück und versucht zu erfahren,
     wem die einzelnen Dinge gehören:

A: Is this (Silvia)'s (book)?
B: Yes, it's (Silvia)'s (book).
C: No, it isn't (Silvia)'s (book).
A: Is this ...?

B10 👥 *Ask and answer.*

A: Is ... going to ...?
B: No, he isn't. He's ... to ...
      No, she isn't. She's ... to ...

1   Madur - John's house - Kim's house
     A: Is Madur going to John's house?
     B: No, she isn't. She's going to Kim's house.

2   Grant - Len's house - the club
3   Kim - Portsmouth - Portchester
4   Mark - the computer shop - the television shop
5   Madur - Grant's club - Kim's club
6   Alec - Portsmouth - the farm
7   Rita - the club - the film
8   Mr Christian - the film - the club

B11 👥 *What are they saying?*

1   *Grant:*   Are you ...ing with Sam?
                (play with Sam)
     Len: No, I'm not. I'm ...ing Mr Christian.
                (help Mr Christian)
2   *Grant:*   Are you ...? (help Mr Christian)
     Len: No, ... I'm ... (wash Skipper)
3   *Grant:*   Are you ...? (play with your pets)
     Len   No, ... (talk to Mr Christian)
4   *Grant:*   Are you ...? (wash Skipper)
     Len: No, ... (play with Sam)

B12 *What are they saying?*

me - you - it

I'm helping ...

Help ..., please.

That's your tea, Jim. Take ...

Please help ..., Mary.

Yes, Miss Jackson. I'm listening to ...

B13 *Words: what are they doing?*

a) He's playing.   d) She's helping.
b) She's shopping.   e) She's washing.
c) He's talking.

B14 *Let's say it.*

[eɪ]

1 Take, play, name, Jane, game, table, say, they, **eigh**t.
2 Take the game, Jane. Play the game, Jane.
3 What's your name? - Jane.
4 They've got **eigh**t games.
5 The games are on the table.

[ɪə]

1 **H**ere, d**ear**, we'**re**, n**ear**.
2 Hello. We'**re h**ere.
3 Oh d**ear**! You'**re h**ere.
4 Oh d**ear**! The monkey is n**ear**.
5 Is the monkey n**ear h**ere?

C

1 Fragen und sagen, wie spät es ist

What's the time, please?	*Wie spät ist es, bitte?*
It's **one** o'clock.	*Es ist **ein** Uhr.*
It's **half past five**.	*Es ist **halb sechs**.*

`01:00`   `05:30`

2 Verlaufsform (Present Progressive)
Fragen und sagen, was jemand gerade jetzt tut

What are you doing?	**I'm helping** this bird.
	(I am)
What's Len doing?	**He's playing** with Skipper.
(What is he)	(He is)
What's mum doing?	**She's shopping**.
(What is she)	(She is)

Are you washing the vegetables?	Yes, I am./No, I'm not.
Is he listening?	Yes, he is./No, he isn't.
Is she buying a pen?	Yes, she is./No, she isn't.

tak**e** – taking	sho**p** – sho**pp**ing
writ**e** – writing	si**t** – si**tt**ing

3 's-Genitiv ('s-Genitive)

Skipper is Len**'s** dog.	*Skipper ist Lens Hund.*
That's Madur**'s** book.	*Das ist Madurs Buch.*

D

D1 ii Act the scene

A: Begrüße B. Frage B, ob seine Schwester/
    ihre Schwester zu Hause ist.

B: Sage, sie ist nicht zu Hause.

A: Frage B, was sie macht. Frage, ob sie
    gerade unterwegs zum Club ist.

B: Sage nein. Sage, sie kauft ein.

A: Frage B, wie es ihm/ihr selbst geht.

B: Sage, dass es dir gut geht.
    Sage, dass du deiner Mutter hilfst.

A: Sage, dass das sehr nett ist.

B: Frage A, was er/sie macht.

A: Sage, du gehst jetzt in den Club.
    Verabschiede dich.

B: Verabschiede dich.

D2 London's burning

Listen to the song and sing it.

LONDON'S BURNING (Traditional song)

London's burning,

London's burning,

Fetch the engines,

Fetch the engines,

Fire, fire,

Fire, fire,

Pour on water,

Pour on water.

engine   = *hier: Feuerwehrwagen*
to pour on = *draufschütten*

D3 📼 How's Sam?

1 *Listen to the cassette.*
2 *What's right: A or B?*

A

Mr. Christian.
Get Sam, please.

B

Mr Christian.
Get Sam, please.

D4 Classroom talk

Please read.

1. *Who has got what?*

The monkey   has got a ...,   a ... and a ...
The bird
The dog
The clown·
The professor

2. ii *Let's make people and talk about them.*

A: Is it a man or a woman?

B: It's a ...

A: What's his/her name?

B: His/Her name is ...

A: Is he/she ...ing?

B: Yes, he/she is.
       No, he/she isn't.

3 *Find twelve English words!*

BOTOJAKNAMLUGIRLOITUNTRISIONOMOVIBATOWNMOMALI
SOPENCILSOSOANOSUGARUIUIILOTILLABINPOESARARYBXN
MAARATARUARUSPASPORTONIPLEASEGUVEMOWINDOWEEM
TANKUWERYMUSHDOORAGWRITEOBIRDUIMWASHAGARETIYXRI
OLLOLLMONKEYASPLOSEHOMEYAPSTREETIGTENONEYOOTIVTZE

4 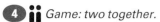 *Game: two together.*

1 Macht euch das oben abgebildete Kartenspiel.
2 *A* hat die roten Karten, *B* die blauen.
   A legt eine Karte auf den Tisch,
   B legt eine Karte mit einem Wort dazu,
   das sich auf das Wort von *A* reimt.
3 Wenn das Wortpaar richtig ist, legt
   B eine neue Karte heraus, sonst
   bleibt *A* an der Reihe.
4 Wer zuerst keine Karten mehr hat,
   hat gewonnen.

5 *Make a poster!*

1 Look at German newspapers
   and magazines.
2 Find English words.
3 Make a poster.

6 *Let's make a*  *Christmas card.*

1 Nimm ein festes weißes Papier und falte es
   in der Mitte.
2 Male etwas Weihnachtliches auf die erste
   Seite, z.B.:
   einen Weihnachtsbaum (a Christmas tree)
   den Weihnachtsmann (Father Christmas)
3 Auf die Innenseite kommt ein Weihnachts-
   oder Neujahrsgruß:
   Happy Christmas
   Merry Christmas
   Happy New Year
   A Merry Christmas and a Happy New Year
4 Nun fehlt noch die Anrede und dein eigener
   Name:
   To ... from ...

7 Now listen to the song and sing it.

We wish you a Merry Christmas,

We wish you a Merry Christmas,

We wish you a Merry Christmas,
and a Happy New Year.

A Christmas Carol

At home

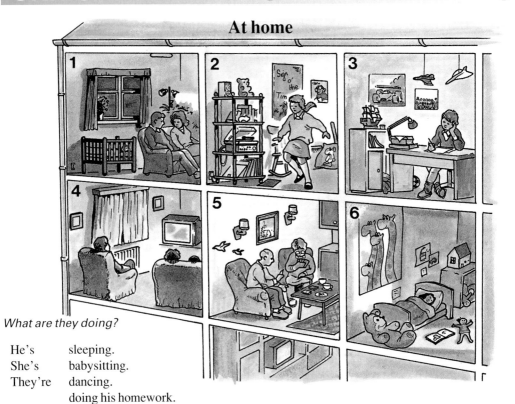

What are they doing?

He's	sleeping.
She's	babysitting.
They're	dancing.
	doing his homework.
	playing cards.
	watching television.

A

Friday evening phone calls

Part 1

Kim:	Hello, Grant. I'm going to the club now. Are you coming, too?
Grant:	No, I'm not. Sorry.
Kim:	Are you doing your homework?
Grant:	No, I'm not.
Kim:	What are you doing, then?
Grant:	I'm babysitting with Rita.
Kim:	Oh, your little brother. Boring!
Grant:	Oh, it's all right. He's asleep. We're watching TV. Come over here.
Baby:	Waaaaaa!
Kim:	No, thanks.

→ **A1**

Part 2

Pat:	Hello, Kim.
Kim:	Hello, Pat. I'm going to the club now. What about you?
Pat:	No, I'm not coming. Sorry, I'm doing my homework.
Kim:	You aren't coming! But what about the film?
Pat:	Oh, yes. What time is the film?
Kim:	It's at six o'clock.
Pat:	Oh dear, no. Sorry, Kim. Ask Grant.
Kim:	No, he isn't coming. He's babysitting.

Part 3 → Ⓐ2

Alec:	Hello.
Kim:	Hello, Alec. Are you coming to the club? Pat and Grant aren't coming.
Alec:	Oh, two elephants!
Kim:	Two elephants?
Alec:	Yes. They're in the street.
Kim:	What? What are they doing?
Alec:	Guess!
Kim:	They're washing your windows.
Alec:	No, they aren't. They're dancing.
Kim:	Dancing?
Alec:	Oh no! Now, they're coming into our garden. They're eating the flowers.
Kim:	Give them a banana.
Alec:	I haven't got a banana. Oh, now dad is in the garden. He's giving them an apple.
Kim:	Are they eating it?
Alec:	Yes, they are. Oh, now they're going.
Kim:	Listen, Alec. Forget the elephants. Are you coming to the club?
Alec:	Oh, yes.

Ⓐ1 *What's right?* → Ⓐ3

Kim	is	doing their homework.
Grant	isn't	going to the club.
Rita and Grant	are	watching TV.
Grant's brother	aren't	babysitting.
		asleep.

Ⓐ2 *What's right?*

Kim	is	going to the club.
Pat	isn't	doing his/her
Grant		homework.
		babysitting.

Ⓐ3 *What's right?*

Kim	is	washing windows.
Alec	isn't	eating an apple.
Mr Ross	are	giving the elephants an apple.
The elephants	aren't	dancing.
		going to the club.

B

B1 *What are they saying?*

1 dance
   We're dancing.
2 do - my homework
   I'm ...
3 help - my mother
4 play with - our computer
5 wash - the dog
6 listen to - a cassette

B2 *What are they saying?*

Kim: What are you doing, Alec?
Alec: Guess!
Kim: You're doing your homework.
Alec: No, I'm not doing my homework.
Kim: You're babysitting.
Alec: No, ...
Kim: You're watching TV.
Alec: No, ...
Kim: You're playing with the dog.
Alec: No, ...
Kim: You're washing the dog.
Alec: No, ...
Kim: Oh, you're helping your mother.
Alec: No, ...
Kim: What are you doing, then?
Alec: I'm watching elephants!

B3 *Play the game.*

Einer von euch *(A)* spielt etwas vor, ohne ein
Wort zu sagen. Die anderen müssen raten,
was er/sie macht.

B: You're ...
A: No, I'm not.
C: You're ...
A: Yes, I am. That's right.

shop   sit down   read   wash   watch ...   play   close   listen to   buy   write

cassette   computer   pet   window   television   game   door   tea   magazine   cup ...   stereo   vegetables

You're doing your homework!
No, I'm not.
You're washing a cup.
That's right!

B4 Talk about the people.

1 Grant isn't going to the club.(go -)
  He's watching television. (watch +)
2 Kim ... (babysit -)
  She ... to the club. (go +)
3 Grant's brother ... television. (watch -)
  He ... (sleep +)
4 Pat ... to the club. (go -)
  She ... her homework. (do +)
5 Kim ... her homework. (do -)
  She ... to the club. (go +)
6 Grant ... to the club. (go -)
  He ... (babysit +)

B5 Ask and answer.

1 A: What time is the German class?
  B: It's at half past ten.

3
2
4
2.00 game
1
4.00 club
8.30 quiz
10.30 German class
6.00 film   5

B6 Talk about the people and pets.

1 They're babysitting.
2 They're ...

B7 What are they saying?

1 A: do - come here?
  B: No - go into - garden.
  A: What are they doing now? Are they
      coming here?
  B: No, they aren't coming here. They're
      going into the garden.
2 A: do - look at - house?
  B: No - look at - flowers.
3 A: do - take - flowers?
  B: No - look at - house.
4 A: do - go into - house?
  B: No - go to - window.
5 A: do - go into - house?
  B: No - look at - door.
6 A: do - go into - house?
  B: Yes - go into - house.

B8 What are they saying?

they - them

1 Look at the elephants. ...'re in the garden!
2 Yes, look at ...! ...'re eating the flowers.
3 Look. Alec and his father. ...'re in the
  garden, too.
4 Yes. The elephants are looking at ...
5 Now ...'re giving ... an apple.
6 Yes and now ...'re going.
7 Who, Alec and his father? - No, the
  elephants. ...'re going.

B9   Let's say it.

[ɔ]

1 Teacher, father, mother, sister, clever,
   elephant, banana, a bag, German, Wilson.
2 Clever teacher, clever mother!
3 Look! A banana in a bag.
4 Mr Wilson isn't German.
5 We haven't got German bananas.
   No, our bananas are American.

[θ]

1 Thing, thanks, thank you.
2 Thank you, thanks, thing.
3 Thanks, thing, thank you.
4 Oh, thank you. Oh, thanks. A thing in a bag.

C

1 Fragen und sagen, wann etwas stattfindet

What time is the film?   *Um wie viel Uhr beginnt der Film?*
It's **at** five o'clock.   *Um fünf Uhr.*

2 What about?

What about the film?   *Was ist mit dem Film?/Und der Film?*
What about you?   *Und du?/Was ist mit dir?*

3 Verlaufsform (Present Progressive)
Fragen und sagen, was mehrere Personen gerade jetzt tun

Grant, Rita, **what are you doing?**   **We're shopping.**
      (We are)
What are they doing?   **They're dancing.**
      (They are)

Are you two **doing** your homework?   Yes, we are./No, we aren't.
Are they helping you?   Yes, they are./No, they aren't.

4 Verlaufsform (Present Progressive)

I'm shopping.   **I'm not shopping.**
You're helping me.   **You aren't helping** me.
He's doing his homework.   **He isn't doing** his homework.
She's doing her homework.   **She isn't doing** her homework.
We're playing cards.   **We aren't playing** cards.
You're watching TV.   **You aren't watching** TV.
They're looking at the house.   **They aren't looking** at the house.

come   –   coming   babysit   –   babysitting
dance   –   dancing   get   –   getting
give   –   giving   put   –   putting

D1 My birthday

Read the texts.

My birthday

1 We're having breakfast. Mum is giving me her present.

2 My friends are singing 'Happy birthday'.

3 I'm visiting my grandmother. We're eating cake.

4 I'm going to the cinema with my friends.

5 This is my party. We're dancing.

6 It's ten o'clock. I'm going to bed.

D2 iii Your friends

1 *Take photos of your family or friends to school.*
2 *Write down what they are doing.*

This is Tanja. She's playing with her dog.

Ask your teacher for more words!

D3 iii Act the scene

A: Begrüße B. Erzähle, dass du in den Club gehst. Frage, ob B auch kommt.

B: Sage, dass du nicht mitkommst.

A: Frage, was B macht.

B: Sage, du machst deine Hausaufgaben. Sage, A soll C fragen.

A: Sage okay. Verabschiede dich.

A: Begrüße C. Erzähle, dass du in den Club gehst. Frage, ob C auch kommt.

C: Sage, dass du nicht mitgehst.

A: Frage, ob C seine/ihre Hausaufgaben macht.

C: Sage, dass du gerade nicht Hausaufgaben machst. Sage, dass du mit dem Hund spielst.

A: Sage, das ist nett. Frage, wie der Hund heißt.

C: Sage, wie der Hund heißt. Sage, dass deine Mutter kommt. Verabschiede dich.

A: Verabschiede dich.

1 ‖ *Ask and answer.*

where - what time - how many - what - how old

1 *A:* ...'s Kim?   *B:* She's at the club.
2 *A:* ...'s that in English?   *B:* It's a pen.
3 *A:* ... televisions have you got?   *B:* I've got two.
4 *A:* ... are you?   *B:* I'm ten.
5 *A:* ... is your friend?   *B:* He's fourteen.
6 *A:* ... are the cups?   *B:* They're in the cupboard.
7 *A:* ... sweets have you got?   *B:* I've got three.
8 *A:* ... is the computer club?   *B:* At half past five.

2 *Talk about the Patels and the Harmans.*

mother - father - daughter - son - sister - brother

1 Mr Patel – Ramesh   3 Madur – Ramesh   6 Mrs Patel – Ramesh
   Mr Patel is Ramesh's father. 4 Madur – Mr Patel   7 Mark – Mr Harman
2 Ramesh – Madur   5 Ramesh – Mr Patel   8 Mrs Harman – Mark

3 *Write the comic.*

Father: Ogg - Is - doing his homework - ?
Mother: No, - isn't - doing his homework - he - .
Father: What's - doing - he - ?
Mother: Look - !

Father: Ogg - , - here - come - !
you - What - are - doing - ?
Ogg: I'm - my bird - with - playing - .
Mother: What's - name - his - ?
Ogg: Yamak - .
Mother: Ogg - , - make - tea - the - .

Mother: You - the tea - making - aren't - .
You're - playing - .
Yamak: We - playing - aren't - .
We're - the tea - making - .
Mother: Ogg - , - Yamak - wash - .
Ogg: Okay - .

Mother: Are - Yamak - washing - you - ?
Ogg: Yes, - washing - I'm - Yamak - .
Father: What - doing - are - they - ?
Mother: Ogg - washing - is - Yamak - .

→ *Start like this:*

1 *Father:* Is Ogg doing his homework?
Mother: No, ...

Father: What's - doing - Yamak - ?
he - Is - asleep - ?
Ogg: Yes, - asleep - he's - .
Father: And - you - what - are - doing - ?
Ogg: babysitting - I'm - .

4 *What's the time, please?*

1 It's ...
2 ...

5 *What's **"elephant"**? Write the right word.*

1 It's half past *elephant*.
2 I'm watching *elephant*.
3 Grant has got a flat *elephant*.
4 The cups are in the *elephant*.
5 Portsmouth is a big British *elephant*.
6 What's that in *elephant*, please?
7 I'm going to the *elephant* now.

The sports centre

come to **THE MOUNTBATTEN CENTRE** and play

SQUASH
VOLLEYBALL
FOOTBALL
BASKETBALL
TENNIS
!!! NEW !!! JUDO CLUB !!! FREE !!!

YOUR SPORTS CENTRE IN ALEXANDRA PARK

What are the sports?

1 Number one is football.
2 Number two ...
3 ...

1   2   3   4   5   6

A

The judo club

Part 1

Pat: Hey, Kim! Where are you going?

Kim: I'm going to the judo club.

Pat: Judo? Is there a judo club here?

Kim: Yes, there is.
At the Mountbatten Centre.

Pat: Oh! That's new.

Alec: The Mountbatten Centre.
What's that?

Pat: A sports centre.
They've got volleyball and basketball.

Kim: And there's a squash club, too.

Alec: Squash! Great!
What about swimming?

Kim: There isn't a swimming pool.

Alec: What a pity!

→ **A1**

Part 2

Alec: Are you good at basketball, Kim?

Kim: I'm all right. What about you?

Alec: I'm not bad at it. I'm good at tennis.
Can you play tennis, too?

Kim: No, not really. But judo is fun.
Hey, Pat. Come to the judo club, too.

Pat: That's a good idea!
Let's ask my father.
Come with us, Alec.

Alec: I can't. Sorry.
I've got a lot of homework.

→ **A2**

Part 3

Pat:	Dad, there's a new judo club at the Mountbatten Centre. Kim is going now. Can I go, too?
Mr Miller:	To a judo club? No, you can't, Pat. I'm sorry. Judo is for boys.
Pat:	Oh, dad!

→ A3

Part 4

Kim:	They've got judo for boys and girls, Mr Miller.
Mr Miller:	Are there two clubs?
Kim:	No, there aren't. There's only one, for boys and girls.
Mr Miller:	No, Pat. You can't go. Judo is dangerous.
Pat:	No, it isn't, dad. And there are judo teachers at the centre.
Mr Miller:	You can't go. It's expensive.
Kim:	No, it isn't, Mr Miller. It's free.
Pat:	Yes, and Kim can go. Oh, please, dad!
Kim:	Yes, please, Mr Miller. Can Pat go, please?
Mr Miller:	Well, all right, Pat. You can go.
Pat:	Great! Thanks, dad! Come on, Kim.
Kim:	Thank you, Mr Miller.

→ A4

A1 *What's right?*

There's	a	swimming pool	at the sports
There isn't		squash club	centre.
		judo club	

A2 *What's right?*

Is	Alec	good at	basketball?	Yes, he is.
	Kim		tennis?	Not really.
				He's not bad.
				She's all right.

A3 *What's missing?*

Pat:	Can I go to the ..., dad?
Mr Miller:	No, you can't. ... is for ...
Pat:	...

A4 *What's right?*

There	is	two judo clubs.
	are	one judo club.
		an expensive judo club.
		a free judo club.
		judo teachers.

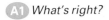

B1 ▮▮ *Ask and answer.*

A:　Is there a (squash) club at the sports centre?
B:　Yes, there is.
　　No, there isn't.

B2 ▮▮ *Ask and answer.*

A:　Are there (four) TVs in the shop?
B:　Yes, there are.
　　No, there aren't. There are (three) TVs.

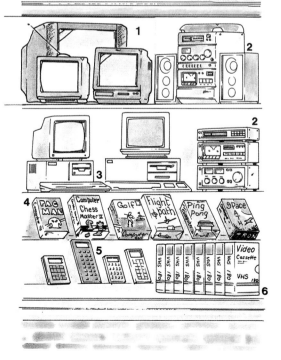

B3 *Ask and answer.*

1　Is there a table in the room?
2　Are there two chairs in the room?
3　... a bird in the room?
4　... three dogs in the room?
5　... a television in the room?
6　... two clocks in the room?
7　... two school bags in the room?
8　... a computer in the room?
9　... a telephone in the room?
10　... two beds in the room?

Yes, there is.　　　　Yes, there are.
No, there isn't.　　　No, there aren't.

B4 *What are they saying?*

1 There's a (monkey) in the old house.
2 There are ...
3 ...

There's a ...

And there are ...

B5  *Now you.*

A: In our class there's (a blackboard).
B: In our class there are ...
C: ...

B6  *Now you.*

A: Are you good at (football)?

B: I'm not bad.   Oh, I'm not very good.

A: Good. Come   That's okay. Come
     and play with us.   and play with us.

     B: Okay.

football
squash volleyball *basketball ...*
          judo

B7  *Now you.*

A: Can you play ...?

B: Yes, I can.   No, I can't.

A: Good. Come   That's okay. Come
     and play with us.   and play with us.

     B: Okay.

     football   squash
tennis   basketball   volleyball ...

B8  *Now you.*

A: Have you got (a rubber)?

B: Yes, I have.

A: Can I have it, please?

B: Yes, you can.   No, you can't.
     Here you are.   I'm sorry.

     pencil   biro
              rubber ...

B9 *Talk about Pat.*

1 Pat can go to Kim's house.
2 Pat ...
3 ...
4 ...
5 Pat can't ...
6 Pat ...
7 ...

Yes, you can.

No, you can't.

1 go to Kim's house
2 watch the quiz
3 go to Alec's house
4 phone Kim
5 go to the judo club
6 listen to the stereo
7 watch TV

B10 *Ask and answer.*

1 Can you come to the club?

A: | Can you come to the club? |
↓
B: Let's ask my mother.

B: Can I go to the club, mum?

C: | Yes, you can. | | No, you can't. |
↓   ↓
A: | Well, can you come? |
↓   ↓
B: Yes, I can.   No, I can't.

A: | Great! | | What a pity! |

2 Can you come to the park?
3 Can you come to the sports centre?
4 Can you come to the football club?
5 Can you come to the swimming pool?
6 Can you come to the squash club?
7 Can you come to the judo club?

B11 *Words: please complete.*

at - for - to

1 *Kim:* Are you good ... tennis, Pat?
2 *Pat:* Dad, there's a new judo club ...
the Mountbatten Centre.
3 *Pat:* Can I go ... the club, dad?
4 *Mr Miller:* Judo is ... boys.

B12 *Let's say it.*

[eə] There, where, chair, their.
[ɑː] Are, car, basketball, Alexandra Park, father.

1 There's a basketball club at the Mountbatten Centre.
2 Come and play volleyball and basketball. Where? - At Alexandra Park.
3 Where are the chairs, father? - There.

[juː]

1 You, computer, music, unit, new.
2 Are you new here?
3 Is that a new unit?
4 Is that your new computer?
5 Is that your computer music?

B13 *Say the rhyme.*

There's the church,   There's the steeple,

Open the door, And there are the people.

church = *Kirche*
steeple = *Kirchturm*

1 There is - there are

There's a judo club at the sports centre.
(There is)

Es gibt einen Judoclub im Sportzentrum.

There are good clubs at the sports centre.

Es gibt gute Clubs im Sportzentrum.

There isn't a swimming pool.
(There is not)

Es gibt kein Schwimmbecken.

There aren't two judo clubs.
(There are not)

Es gibt keine zwei Judoclubs.

Is there a squash club?

Yes, **there is.**

Is there a swimming pool?

No, **there isn't.**

Are there two football clubs?

Yes, **there are.**

Are there two judo clubs?

No, **there aren't.**

2 Sagen und fragen, wie gut man etwas kann

I'm **good at** tennis.

Ich spiele gut Tennis.

I'm **all right at** football.

Ich spiele ganz gut Fußball.

I'm **not bad at** judo.

Ich bin nicht schlecht in Judo.

Are you **good at** volleyball?

Yes, I am.

No, I'm not.

Not really.

3 Fragen und sagen, ob man etwas kann oder darf: can

Can you play tennis?

***Kannst du** Tennis spielen?*

Can I go to the judo club?

***Darf ich** in den Judoclub gehen?*

Can I go to the swimming pool?

Yes, **you can.**

No, **you can't.**

I	**can**	come.	I	**can't**	come.
You			You	(cannot)	
He			He		
She			She		
We			We		
They			They		

4 Um etwas bitten: can

Can I have your pencil, please?

***Kann ich** bitte deinen Bleistift haben?*

Can you help me, please?

***Kannst du** mir bitte helfen?*

D1 📼 **At the judo club**

1 Listen to the cassette.

2 Please answer.

a) Where are Kim and Pat?   c) Is he good at judo?
b) What's the boy's name?   d) Is Kim good at judo?

D2 **Activities in Portsmouth - activities in your town**

1 What can you do at the Mountbatten Centre?

You can ...
There's a ...
There are ...
...

2 What can you do in your town?

I can go to ...
We can play ...
There's a ...
There are ...
...

D3 **A survey**

1 👥 *Here's a survey of the Paulsgrove people. Ask your partner questions about the survey.*

A: Is (Pat) good at (squash)?
B: Yes, he/she is.
     He/She's not bad.
     Not really.

	Kim	Pat	Alec	Mark	Grant	John
Football	*	*	*	**	***	**
Basketball	*	***	***	***	**	**
Volleyball	***	***	***	***	***	*
Squash	*	*	*	*	**	***
Judo	***	**	**	*	***	**
Tennis	**	***	***	**	***	**

*** = good   ** = not bad   * = not very good

2 👥👥 *Now you. Make a survey of your group. Ask your partners and write the answers in a survey.*

A: (Silvia), can you play (volleyball)?
B: Yes, I can./No, I can't.
A: Are you good at it?
B: ...

3 Look at your survey. Speak about your group. Start like this:

In my group there are (six) people.
(Two) are good at ...
(Silvia) is not bad at ...
...

The box of nuts

It's a nice summer day in the village of Crickwood. Mick, Pam and Dave, three hamsters, are sitting in a big tree near Joe's farm.

Mick: There are wonderful nuts in a box on the table in the kitchen.
Dave: Really? Nuts are nice!
Pam: Nuts are very nice! Let's get them.
Dave: What about the dog?
Mick: He's in the fields with Joe.
Pam: The problem is - how can we get into the kitchen?
Mick: Let me think. The key is always under the doormat. We can put the key in the lock. Then we can hang on it and open the door.
Pam: Great. Let's run.
Mick: Okay.
Dave: Let's go!

It's easy - and now the clever hamsters have got the nuts. They're going to the pond.

Pam: Let's eat the nuts under the tree near the pond.
Mick: That's a good idea!
Dave: Give me the box.

But the big box is full and very heavy.

Pam: Look! Dave is very tired. He's dropping the nuts in the grass.
Mick: Yes. Well, they're his nuts. Our nuts are in the box.

Now they're under the tree near the pond.

Dave: I'm tired and hungry. Let's eat the nuts now.
Pam: I'm sorry, Dave. The nuts in the box are for Mick and me. Your nuts are in the grass.
Dave: In the grass? Oh, no! Well, all right.

Pam: Very nice nuts.
Mick: Very, very nice nuts. What's Dave doing? Is he looking for his nuts?
Pam: I can't see him.
Mick: I can. Look!
Pam: Oh yes! Dave is in a nut tree. Look at all the nuts!
Mick: Yes, and look now. Here's Joe's dog. Quick! Run, Pam! Run!

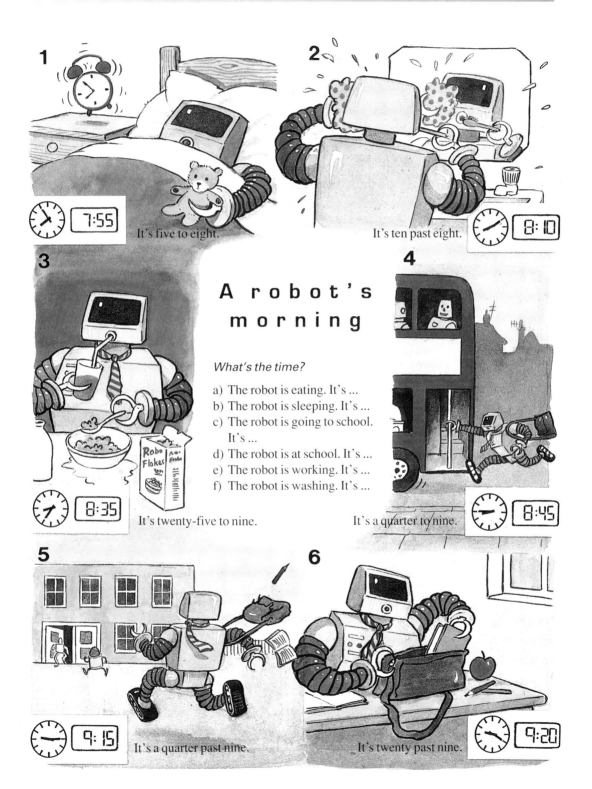

1

7:55

It's five to eight.

2

8:10

It's ten past eight.

3

8:35

It's twenty-five to nine.

A robot's morning

What's the time?

a) The robot is eating. It's ...
b) The robot is sleeping. It's ...
c) The robot is going to school. It's ...
d) The robot is at school. It's ...
e) The robot is working. It's ...
f) The robot is washing. It's ...

4

8:45

It's a quarter to nine.

5

9:15

It's a quarter past nine.

6

9:20

It's twenty past nine.

A

The super
robot

Part 1

Pat:	What's the time, Kim?
Kim:	It's ten to four.
Pat:	What time is the basketball club?
Kim:	It's at half past five.

Mark:	Listen. My father has got a robot.
Pat:	A robot?
Mark:	Yes, he's very clever.
Pat:	Clever?
Kim:	Oh, yes, he's very clever. He speaks French and German and ...
Pat:	Yes, and he lives at your house. And he sleeps in your room and ...
Mark:	Oh, shut up! He's at my dad's shop. Come and see.
Kim:	Okay, Mark.

→ **A1**

Part 2

Mark:	Look! He can sit down. Robot, sit down!
Kim:	Wow! You're right.
Mark:	And he can stand up. Robot, stand up!
Pat:	He's great!
Mark:	Now listen to this! Robot, what's the time?
Robot:	It's a quarter past four. A cup of tea, please.
Kim:	He's right. The robot talks.
Mark:	He speaks French, too. Bonjour, robot.
Robot:	Bonjour.
Kim:	Ha, ha! This is super, Mark. What's his name?
Mark:	Robby Rob.
Mark:	Look! He walks, too. Robot, walk!
Pat:	Ha, ha!
Mark:	Help! Come here, robot!

→ **A2**

Part 3

Robot: Fish and chips, please.
Man: Aargh!
Robot: Good afternoon. Can I dance with you, please?
Old lady: Oh, yes. Thank you. This is fun.
Pat: Look, Kim, he can dance, too!
Robot: You're nice.
Old lady: Thank you. And you're nice, too.
Kim: He likes her.
Pat: And she likes him.

→ A3

A1 *What's right?*

Pat's	father	has got a robot	at home.
Mark's			at his shop.
Kim's			

A3 *What's missing?*

dance - likes - nice

Old lady: The robot is ...
           He can ...
           He ... me.

A2 *What's right?*

The robot	can	sit down.
	can't	speak German.
		speak French.
		walk.

A4 *Can you say the numbers?*

Numbers II

13 thirteen	21 twenty-one	31 thirty-one	40 forty
14 fourteen	22 twenty-two	32 thirty-two	50 fifty
15 fifteen	23 twenty-three	etc.	60 sixty
16 sixteen	24 twenty-four		70 seventy
17 seventeen	25 twenty-five		80 eighty
18 eighteen	26 twenty-six		90 ninety
19 nineteen	27 twenty-seven		
20 twenty	28 twenty-eight		
	29 twenty-nine		100 a hundred
	30 thirty		one hundred

B

B1 👥 *Ask and answer.*

1 A: What's the time, please?
   B: It's five past ten.
2 ...

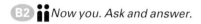

1	10.05	7	11.30
2	9.20	8	8.25
3	4.15	9	7.15
4	6.45	10	2.35
5	1.10	11	6.55
6	3.45	12	5.40

B2 👥 *Now you. Ask and answer.*

A: What time is your   breakfast?
                         teatime?
                         class?
                         club?
                         ...?

B: (Breakfast) is at ...

B3 *Talk about the people and pets.*

eats - likes - lives - plays - speaks - walks

1 Alec Ross ... in Portsmouth.
2 John ... squash at the Mountbatten Centre.
3 Grant ... football.
4 The super robot ...
5 Mr Christian ... bananas.
6 The super robot ... English and French.

Riddle

What goes up when the rain comes down?

An umbrella.

B4 *Talk about the people.*

1
This is Mark Harman.
He lives in a big house.
He's got a stereo and a television.
He plays football.
He likes computer games.

2
- Alec Ross
- in Paulsgrove
- Scottish
- volleyball
- cars

3
- Kim Fielding
- in Paulsgrove
- small house
- judo club

4
- Len Bignall
- Portchester
- old house
- dog, monkey
- the dog's name
- the monkey's name
- tea

B5 *Now you. Talk about a friend.*

This is (Tanja).
(She) lives in ...
(She) likes ...
(She) plays ...
(She) ...

B6 *Talk about the people and pets.*

him - her

1 Kim is nice. Let's visit ...
2 Alec is okay. Let's ask ...
3 Madur is ill. Let's visit ...
4 Rick likes Kim and she likes ...
5 Kim likes Rick and he likes ...
6 Sam is Mr Christian's friend. He plays
   with ...

B7 *What are they saying?*

him - her - us

She likes ...

He likes ...

Come with ...

Play with ...

She likes ...

B8 *Words: good or bad?*

an awful dog - a clever game - a great teacher -
a dangerous sport - a happy class - a nice woman -
a super stereo - a boring film

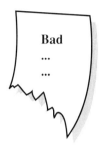

Good	Bad
...	...
...	...

B9 *Words: odd man out.*

1	2	3
come	listen	talk
listen	look	write
walk	watch	speak

B10 *Words: two together.*

1 **ask**   5 speak
2 come   6 write
3 give   7 **answer**
4 go   8 take

B11 📼 *Let's say it.*

[w] **W**alk, **wh**at, **w**e, **wh**ere, **w**indow.
[r] **R**obot, f**r**iend, F**r**ench, ve**r**y, w**r**ite, **r**ight,
     g**r**eat.

1 Look! **Wh**at a g**r**eat **r**obot!
2 **Wh**ere are **w**e going?
   We're **w**alking to the club **w**ith the **r**obot.
3 The **r**obot is w**r**iting to a F**r**ench f**r**iend.
4 Forget your pets, Len.
   We've got a g**r**eat new **r**obot here.

[ɔɪ]

1 This is a b**oy**.
2 This is a t**oy**.
3 This is a b**oy**'s t**oy**.
4 This is a t**oy** b**oy**.

B12 *Say the rhyme.*

In the morning at eight o'clock,
Rat-tat-tat! The postman's knock.
Mary Carey opens the door,
One letter, two letters, three letters, four.
Two for mum and one for dad,
One for Mary, she is glad!

C

1 Die Uhrzeit (The Time)

1 It's eight o'clock.
2 It's five past eight.
3 It's a quarter past eight.
4 It's twenty past eight.

5 It's half past eight.
6 It's twenty-five to nine.
7 It's a quarter to nine.
8 It's ten to nine.

2 Einfache Gegenwart (Present Simple)
Sagen, was jemand immer, im Allgemeinen oder regelmäßig macht

The super robot **speaks** French.
The old lady often **dances** with the robot.
The bird **lives** in a small house.

He speaks. [-s]
She dances. [- z]
It lives. [-z]

3 Persönliche Fürwörter (Personal Pronouns)

I'm ill. Please visit **me**.
You're ill? Pat can visit **you**.
He's ill. John is visiting **him**.
She's nice. Kim visits **her**.
We're ill. Please visit **us**.
You're ill, Kim and Pat?
    Alec can visit **you**.
They're ill. Grant is visiting **them**.

Ich bin krank. Bitte besuche **mich**.
Du bist krank? Pat kann **dich** *besuchen.*
Er ist krank. John besucht **ihn**.
Sie ist nett. Kim besucht **sie**.
Wir sind krank. Bitte besuche **uns**.
Ihr seid krank, Kim und Pat?
    Alec kann **euch** *besuchen.*
Sie sind krank. Grant besucht **sie**.

(D1) **My friend**

1 Read the letter.

Here's a letter from a reader:

My friend's name is Martin. He's eleven. He's got a big dog. The dog's name is Raffles.

Martin has got a good hobby - computers. He's got a small computer in his room! He plays football and he likes music, too. Martin is good at swimming. He hasn't got a dad at home. His mum is very nice. He's not bad at school.

George B.

2 Now write to the magazine about your friend.

How old is he/she?
Has he/she got a pet?
What are his/her hobbies?
Is he/she good at sports?

What has he/she got in his/her room?
Has he/she got a nice mum and dad?
Is he/she good at school?

D2 Classroom talk

Please read.

D3 ⠿ SCHOOL QUIZ

1 Make notes about a pupil or a teacher.

He/She lives in ...
He/She's ten/eleven/...
He/She plays ... and ...
He/She likes ... and ...
He/She is good at ... and ...
He/She's not bad at ...
He/She's got ...

2 Now tell the class about the person.

3 Now ask the class.

A: Who is it?
Class: Is it (Peter)?
A: No, it isn't.
Class: It's ...
A: Yes, that's right!

1 *What are they saying?*

me - you - him - her - it - us - them

1 Our homework is awful. Let's phone Kim.
   She can help ...
2 Where are the cups? Have you got ...?
3 That's Mr Harman's car. Look at ...
4 That's Pat's house. Let's visit ...

5 Look, they're playing volleyball.
   Hey, Alec, Kim, can we play with ...?
6 Oh, I can't see my pen. Help ..., please.
7 Okay, I can help ... Here it is.
8 Mr Wilson is nice. Let's ask ...

2 iii Act the scene

A: Schlage B vor, ins Schwimmbad zu gehen.

B: Sage, dass das eine gute Idee ist.

A: Frage C, ob er/sie auch mitkommen kann.

C: Schlage vor, deine Mutter zu fragen.

C: Frage D, ob du mitkommen darfst.

D: Sage, dass C mitgehen darf.

D: Sage, dass C nicht mitgehen darf.

B: Frage C, ob er/sie mitkommen darf.

C: Sage, dass du mitkommen darfst.

C: Sage, dass du nicht mitkommen darfst.

B: Drücke deine Freude aus.

B: Drücke dein Bedauern aus.

3 *Talk about Len's friends.*

1 John Roberts
   (Len/friend/Paulsgrove/good bike/squash)
   This is John Roberts. He's Len's friend.
   He lives in Paulsgrove. He's got a good bike
   and he likes squash.
2 Skipper
   (Len/dog/Portchester/sleeps on table/birds)
3 Mr Christian
   (Len/monkey/Castle Street/big cup/
   tea and bananas)

4 **The magic square**

*How many words
can you make?*
1 come
2 nice
3 ...

N	T	O
A	I	M
R	C	E

BRITISH HOUSES

Now you. Talk about the houses.

1 The houses are (nice).
2 The house is …
3 …

Where's Len?

Part 1

Alec:	Tell me about Len, John.
John:	He's an old sailor.
Alec:	An old sailor? How old?
John:	He's sixty-eight. And he's got a monkey.
Alec:	A monkey?
John:	Yes, his name is Mr Christian.

They're always at home. Len works in his garden every afternoon.
Well, he does his shopping sometimes. And Mr Christian often helps him.
And Len goes to his club on Thursdays. Every week.

→ (A1) (A2)

Part 2

Alec: Whose dog is that?
John: That's Skipper. Len's dog.
Hello, Skipper, girl. How are you?

John: Hey, what's the matter, Skipper?

Alec: Where's Len?
John: That's funny. He's always in the garden.
Every afternoon.
Alec: Maybe he isn't at home today.
John: Oh, look, the door is open.

Part 3

John:	What's the matter, Len?
Len:	It's my leg, John.
John:	Oh, is it bad?
Len:	Yes, it's bad today, John. I can't walk. Hmmm, what day is it today?
John:	It's Saturday.
Len:	Oh, dear, oh, dear! It's my shopping day.
Alec:	Well, can we do your shopping, Mr Bignall?
Len:	Len. My name is Len.
Alec:	Okay, Len.
John:	Is that your shopping list?
Len:	Yes, it is. Oh, all right. Thanks. Well, I'd like a packet of tea. A small jar of coffee. And I'd like two tins of dog food. A bottle of milk. Two boxes of matches and a bag of sugar. Oh, yes, and two bananas for Mr Christian. Here's the shopping list, boys.

→ **A3** **A4**

A1 *What's right?*

Len	has got	a monkey.
The monkey's name	is	sixty-eight.
		Mr Christian.

A2 *Len Bignall's week. What's missing?*

1 Len works ... every afternoon.
2 Len and Mr Christian are always ...
3 Len sometimes does ....
4 ... often helps ...
5 Len ... on Thursdays.

A3 *What's right?*

1 Where's Len today?
  a) He's in the garden.
  b) He's in his house.

2 What's the matter?
  a) Len's leg is bad.
  b) The door is open.

3 What day is it today?
  a) It's Thursday.
  b) It's Saturday.

4 On Saturdays Len
  a) does his shopping.
  b) goes to his club.

5 Len
  a) can do the shopping.
  b) can't walk today.

A4 *Write Len's shopping list.*

The parts of the body

Look at Mr Christian and learn the new words.

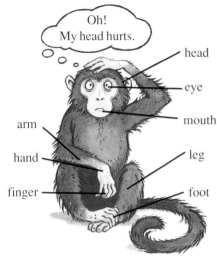

Oh! My head hurts.

head

eye

arm

mouth

hand

leg

finger

foot

A5 👥 Now you.

A: Oh! My foot hurts!
B: Oh! My ... hurts!
C: ...

The days of the week

Can you say the days?

Die Wochentage werden im Englischen immer groß geschrieben.

B

B1 Talk about the people.

1 Kim goes on **Tuesdays** and **Fridays**.
2 Pat ...

Kim	- **judo** and **basketball**
Pat	- volleyball and basketball
Alec	- volleyball
Mark	- football
Grant	- judo and football
John	- squash

MOUNTBATTEN SPORTS CENTRE

Mon	Squash
Tues	Judo
Wed	Football
Thurs	Volleyball
Fri	Basketball
Sat	Squash
Sun	Football

Mon	= Monday	Fri	= Friday
Tues	= Tuesday	Sat	= Saturday
Wed	= Wednesday	Sun	= Sunday
Thurs	= Thursday		

B2 *Talk about the people. It's Saturday.*

1 John **sometimes** does the shopping.
2 He **often** watches television and goes ...
3 He **always** ...
4 Len ...
5 He ...

6 ...
7 Kim ...
8 She ...
9 ...

	do the shopping	work in the garden	watch television	go swimming	play squash
John	*		**	**	***
Len	**	***	*		
Kim	***	*	**	**	

*** = always   ** = often   * = sometimes

B3 *Now you. Talk about your mother and father.*

My mother	often	does the shopping	on Saturdays.
My father	always	goes to town	
He	sometimes	watches television	
She		plays ...	
		works in the garden	
		works at home	
		phones friends	

B4 *Talk about Fuzzy.*

dances - does the shopping - goes swimming - sleeps

1 Fuzzy ... every Tuesday.
2 He ... every ...

3 He ...
4 ...

B5 *Now you. Talk about your mother and father.*

My mother	watches television	every	morning.
My father	goes swimming		afternoon.
He	does the shopping		day.
She	...		

B6 *Ask and answer.*

1 Whose monkey is that?
   It's Len's monkey.

2 Whose house is that?
   It's ... house.

3 ... mother ...?
   ...

4 ... bird ...?
   ...

5 ... sister ...?
   ...

6 ... house ...?
   ...

7 ... computer ...?
   ...

8 ... cup ...?
   ...

B7 *What is she saying?*

Mrs Harman:

I'd like	a	bag(s)	of	coffee.
	two	bottle(s)		dog food.
	...	box(es)		matches.
		jar(s)		milk.
		packet(s)		sugar.
		tin(s)		tea.

B8 *What's the number?*

42	1 **Forty-two**
	2 Twenty-four
27	1 Seventy-two
	2 Twenty-seven
38	1 Eighty-three
	2 Thirty-eight
69	1 Ninety-six
	2 Sixty-nine
76	1 Seventy-six
	2 Sixty-seven
83	1 Eighty-three
	2 Thirty-eight
54	1 Forty-five
	2 Fifty-four
95	1 Fifty-nine
	2 Ninety-five

B9 *Words: odd man out.*

1	2	3
boy	chair	basketball
dog	cup	judo
girl	desk	squash
man	table	tennis

B10  Let's say it.

[uː] Afternoon, who, you, two, do, food.

[æ] Man, matter, Saturday, packet, bag.

1 Good afternoon. Who are you two?

2 What's the matter, Len? Is it Saturday?

3 We can do Len's shopping on Saturday afternoon.

4 I'd like two packets of tea and a bag of sugar.

[f] or [v]?

1 Len's foot is very bad.

2 That's funny. My finger is very bad, too.

3 Football is very good fun.

4 Volleyball is very good fun, too.

C

1 Fragen und sagen, wem etwas gehört

Whose dog is this?

This is Len**'s** dog.

Wessen Hund ist das?/Wem gehört dieser Hund?

Das ist Lens Hund.

2 Sagen, was man haben möchte

I'd like a small packet of tea, please.

We'd like two tins of dog food, please.

Ich möchte bitte ein Päckchen Tee.

Wir möchten bitte zwei Dosen Hundenahrung.

I like bananas.

I'd like two bananas, please.

*= Ich **mag** Bananen.*

*= Ich **möchte** bitte zwei Bananen.*

3 Sagen, wie oft jemand etwas macht

a) Len **works** in his garden **every afternoon**.

  every afternoon

  every day

  every morning

  every Thursday

*Len arbeitet **jeden Nachmittag** in seinem Garten.*

jeden Nachmittag

jeden Tag

jeden Morgen

jeden Donnerstag

b) Len **sometimes does** his shopping.

  Kim **often watches** television.

  John **always plays** squash.

*Len geht **manchmal** einkaufen.*

*Kim sieht **oft** fern.*

*John spielt **immer** Squash.*

c) Grant and John **are often** at Len's house.

  Len **is always** in the garden.

*Grant und John sind **oft** bei Len.*

*Len ist **immer** im Garten.*

4 Sagen, dass jemand etwas regelmäßig an einem bestimmten Tag macht

Len **goes** to his club **on Thursdays**.

***Donnerstags** geht Len in seinen Club.*

5 Aussprache -es

do	–	does	[dʌz]
go	–	goes	[gəʊz]
watch	–	watches	[–ɪz]

one box	–	two boxes	[–ɪz]
one match	–	two matches	[–ɪz]
one hobby	–	two hobbies	[–ɪz]

D °

D1 ⋮⋮⋮ Bingo

1 *Mache dir eine Bingokarte.*

2 *Dein Lehrer oder ein Mitschüler ruft Zahlen aus.*

3 *Wenn du eine Zahl hörst, die du auf deiner Karte hast, kreuze sie an.*

4 *Hast du Kreuze auf allen Zahlen einer Reihe, rufe Bingo.*

5 *Wer als erster Bingo ruft, hat gewonnen.*

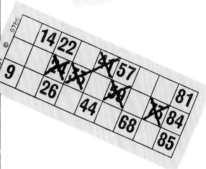

D2 Seven days

Say the rhyme.

Monday, Monday,
One day after Sunday,
Monday is our washing day,
There isn't time for games today.

Tuesday, Tuesday,
Our one–and–one–is–two day,
A lot of work at school today,
A lot of homework we can't play.

Wednesday, Wednesday,
Wednesday is friends' day,
You can come with us and play,
Everybody's here today.

Thursday, Thursday,
Maybe there's a birthday,
Party, presents, cake and then,
Oh, no! It's time for bed again.

Friday, Friday,
Fish and chips for tea today,
No more work till Monday,
It's a very happy day!

Saturday, Saturday,
Where's the list? It's shopping day.
Bananas, apples, biscuits, tea,
And milk and bread to buy today.

Sunday, Sunday,
Hobbies, sport and fun day,
And it's only one day till
Monday, Monday...

1 *Play the poster game.*

1 Nimm eine Zeitschrift und suche Bilder von zehn Gegenständen, von denen du den englischen Namen kennst (car, house, bike, book, computer, television, etc).

2 Schneide diese Bilder aus und klebe sie auf ein großes Papier. So erhältst du ein Poster.

3 Zeige dein Poster einem Mitschüler für ca. eine halbe Minute.

4 Der Mitschüler versucht danach, alle Dinge aufzuschreiben (natürlich auf Englisch!), die er auf deinem Poster gesehen hat.

5 Hat er alle zehn Gegenstände auf seiner Liste, gewinnt er; sonst bist du der Sieger.

2 ⅲ *Find the missing letters.*

1 Suche dir zwei Partner.

2 Jeder von euch denkt sich fünf englische Wörter aus und schreibt sie auf einen Zettel. Setzt dabei an die Stelle eines jeden Selbstlautes ein Sternchen. Das Wort „football" würde z.B. so aussehen: f * * tb * ll.

3 Tauscht nun eure Zettel aus. Derjenige, der als erster die fünf Wörter errät, hat gewonnen.

3 *Can you say the tongue-twisters?*

She sells sea shells

on the sea shore.

Pat placed

Peter's parcel

in the post van.

tongue-twister	=	*Zungenbrecher*
shells	=	*Muscheln*
shore	=	*Strand, Ufer*
placed	=	*legte*
parcel	=	*Päckchen*
post van	=	*Postwagen*

4 *Play the game:*   **Teatime with Len**

Have you got a pawn and a dice ? Play with one to three partners.
You can say: What have you got? It's your turn. Come on. I've got a '1'! It's my turn. I'm the winner!

Your dad phones: "What about your homework? Come home!" Go back to 1. **31**	Skipper says 'Hello'. Move to 34. **32**	Mr Christian has got your cup. Miss two turns. **33**	**34**	**35**	It's teatime. **36**
30	**29**	**28**	**27**	A friend has got a pump. Go on to 34. **26**	You haven't got a pump. Miss a turn. **25**
19	**20**	**21**	**22**	You've got a flat tyre. Go back to 16. **23**	**24**
18	**17**	**16**	**15**	You've got the shopping. Go on to 21. **14**	**13**
7	**8**	Mum: "What about the shopping?" Go back to 3. **9**	**10**	**11**	**12**
6	**5**	"Can I go to Len's house, dad?" "Yes, you can." **4** Go on to 8.	**3**	**2**	Start. Your house. **1**

British money

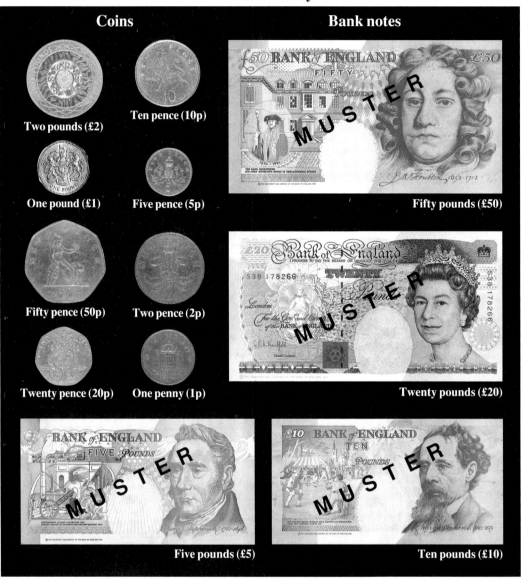

Coins	Bank notes
Two pounds (£2)	
Ten pence (10p)	
One pound (£1)	
Five pence (5p)	Fifty pounds (£50)
Fifty pence (50p)	
Two pence (2p)	
Twenty pence (20p)	
One penny (1p)	Twenty pounds (£20)
	Five pounds (£5)
	Ten pounds (£10)

How much is that? Ask and answer.

A: How much is number (one)?
B: That's ...

£4.32 = four pounds thirty-two/four thirty-two
32p = thirty-two p [pi:]/thirty-two pence [pens]

PAULSGROVE CLUB MAGAZINE

Our shop

by Madur Patel

Our shop - well, it's really my brother's shop - sells newspapers, magazines, cigarettes, sweets, drinks and chocolate. It's an English corner shop really, but we sell Asian food, too, and that's new in Paulsgrove.

Ramesh and I live with our parents. We've got a flat above the shop. Our parents are Indian but Ramesh and I are British. Portsmouth is our home. We love Britain but our parents aren't really happy here.

Ramesh opens the shop at eight in the morning and he only closes it at eight in the evening. People in Paulsgrove like that. "The other shops close at six and we can't buy Asian food in them," they say.

Things are fine really. But there is one problem. I like our corner shop. It's nice and small. But my brother wants a big shop one day.

A1 *What's right?*

1 The Patels sell
2 They sell
3 The Patels live
4 Ramesh and Madur are
5 Their parents are
6 Ramesh and Madur love Britain but
7 Ramesh opens the shop
8 He closes it
9 The other shops close
10 People can do their shopping
11 Ramesh wants

a) a big shop.
b) Asian food, too.
c) at eight in the evening.
d) at eight in the morning.
e) at six in the evening.
f) British.
g) in a flat above the shop.
h) Indian.
i) in the morning or in the evening.
j) newspapers,magazines,cigarettes, sweets, drinks and chocolate.
k) their parents aren't happy.

At the shop

John: Is that all, Alec?
Alec: Tea, coffee, matches, milk, dog food, bananas. Yes, that's all.
John: What about the sugar?
Alec: Oh, yes. A bag of sugar. Here it is.

John: How much is that, Ramesh?
Ramesh: That's £6.45.
John: Here you are.
Ramesh: Thanks. And here's your change. 55p.

A2 *What's right?*

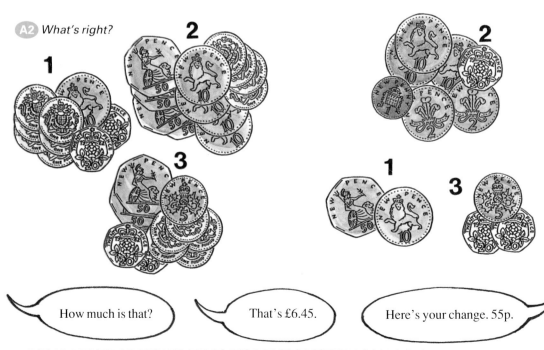

How much is that?   That's £6.45.   Here's your change. 55p.

B1 *Talk about the people.*

do - go - help - like - play - visit

John and Grant are good friends. They ... their homework together. They ... to school together every morning. They've got a nice teacher. They ... football and squash. They ... Kim and Pat. They often ... Len in Portchester. They ... him and his dog and monkey. They ... him in the garden and sometimes ... his shopping.

B2 *What are they saying?*

I	buy	Len in the garden	on Fridays.
We	go	fish and chips	on ....
	help	football	every day.
	play	in my brother's shop	
	work	to my club	
		to the judo club	

	MON	TUES	WED	THURS	FRI	SAT	SUN
Len				*			
Mr Christian	*	*	*	*	*	*	*
Madur						*	
Grant and John							*
Robby Rob					*		
Kim and Pat		*					

B3 *Now you.*

I	often	watch TV	on	Saturdays.
	always	go to the sports centre		Sundays.
	sometimes	visit friends		
		play ...		
		help my mum		
		do the shopping		
		...		

B4 *Now you. Talk about your school.*

On	Mondays	I	come to school at	... o'clock.
	Tuesdays	we	go home from school at	half past ...
	...		go to school from	... to ...

B5 *Now you. Talk about your family.*

My	father	works	from ... to ...
	mother	goes to school	at ...
	brother	comes home	
	sister		

B6 ❙❙ *Talk to your partner.*

1 bottle of milk – two boxes of matches – 41p

A: Good morning. Can I help you?
B: Good morning. I'd like a bottle of milk, please.
A: Is that all?
B: No, I'd like two boxes of matches, please.
A: Here you are.
B: How much is that?
A: That's 41 pence, please.

2 tin of dog food – newspaper – 65p

A: Good morning. Can ...?
B: ... I'd like ..., please.
A: Is that ...?
B: No, ..., please.
A: Here ...
B: How much ...?
A: That's ...

3 packet of tea - six bananas - £1.32

A: ...
B: ...

B7 *Words: food or drink?*

banana - cake - chocolate - coffee - milk -
sweets - tea - vegetables

B8 *Words: two together.*

he	brother	dad	...
she	...	...	mother

B9 ▶️ *Let's say it.*

[əʊ]

1 Is the robot phoning Coco?
2 Is Coco doing his homework? I don't know.
3 Is the robot doing judo? No.
4 Let's go to the robot show!

[æ] or [e]?

1 Let's visit Ramesh in his flat.
2 What's the matter? Tell me. - No, you aren't my friend.
3 Look at that. Your tyre is flat.
4 Who's that? Tell me. - That's Ramesh Patel.

[v] or [w]?

1 Well, that's a very good video.
2 What a good video!
3 We're visiting a very nice woman.
4 We play volleyball every week.

1 Was man beim Einkaufen sagt

Can I help you?	*Kann ich dir/euch helfen?*
I'd like a bottle of mil, please.	*Ich möchte bitte eine Flasche Milch.*
How much is that, please?	*Wie viel macht das, bitte?*
That's £1.50.	*Das macht ein Pfund fünfzig.*
Is that all, please?	*Ist das alles, bitte?*
Here you are.	*Bitte schön.* (beim Überreichen von Waren oder Geld)

2 Einfache Gegenwart (Present Simple)
Sagen, was jemand immer, im Allgemeinen oder regelmäßig macht

I live in a flat.

You always **buy** chocolate.

Ramesh Patel **sells** newspapers and magazines.

We live with our parents.

They get Asian food in Ramesh Patel's shop.

I	live	in a house.	**He**	lives	in a house.
You			**She**		
We			**It**		
They					

D

D1 Picnic day for teddy bears

1 Read the text.

a) Boys and girls and their mothers and fathers like picnics.

b) But teddy bears love them. And every year the teddy bears have their picnic in the wood.

c) It's picnic day for teddy bears.
   They pay their money
   and eat bread and honey.

d) They drink their tea,
   very nice tea.

e) They dance and dance
   (Yes, bears can dance!).

f) In the evening they go home and they're happy little teddy bears.

2 Match the pictures to the sentences.

D2 ▄▄ At the shops

1 Listen to the cassette.
2 Write Coco's shopping list.
3 What's right?

a) Coco goes into the   greengrocer's.
                           newsagent's.
                           supermarket.

b) He wants ... at the ...
   He buys ... at ...
c) The sweets are ...p.
   The apples and bananas are ...p.

D3 Your shop

Write about a shop in your town.
This list can help you.

Shop's name.
Where's the shop?
The shop sells ...
It opens at ...
It closes at ...
I often/sometimes go there.
I go there on ...
I buy ... there.

D4 ▪▪▪ Act the scene

A und *B* sind Kunden.
C ist Verkäufer(in) bzw. Ladenbesitzer(in).
A und *B* machen sich eine Einkaufsliste und
kaufen bei *C* ein.
C legt die Preise fest.

C: Begrüße A und B.

A&B: Begrüßt C.

C: Frage die Kunden nach ihren Wünschen.

A: Nenne die ersten zwei Waren auf deiner
         Liste.

C: Überreiche die Ware.
         Frage, ob das alles ist.

B: Nenne die nächste Ware auf der Liste.

C: Überreiche die Ware.
         Frage, ob das alles ist.

A&B: Geht eure Liste Punkt für Punkt durch,
         während C die Waren überreicht und die
         Preise nennt. Dann sagt, dass das
         alles ist.

C: Sage, wie viel das macht.

A: Überreiche das Geld.

C: Bedanke dich. Verabschiede dich.

A&B: Verabschiedet euch.

The clever crow

It is a lovely morning in spring. Fleet, the fox,
is looking for food.

He sees a nest up in a tree. There is a mother
bird in it with her three baby birds.

5   "Hey, you up there," Fleet shouts.
"Throw down one of your babies."

"No," the mother bird answers.
"Go away, fox, go away."

"Right," Fleet shouts again. "I'm

10   coming up for all four of you."

The mother bird is very
afraid. But there is also a clever
crow in the tree. She shouts, "It's all
right, mother bird. The fox can't

15   come up. He can't climb or fly."

The fox is angry and runs
away.

Then one day he sees the crow. He is hungry! He lies down on the ground and closes his eyes. "Is
the fox dead?" the crow thinks. But she is very clever. "Dead foxes have their eyes open," she

20   shouts. Fleet opens his eyes. "You aren't dead," the crow says. "You're a fool!" She laughs and flies
away. Now Fleet is very angry.

Later he sees the crow again. Now he has got a plan. He lies down on the ground again. The crow
sees him.

"Dead foxes have their eyes open," she shouts. But Fleet is clever. His eyes are closed. The crow

25   comes near, but Fleet's eyes are still closed.

So the crow jumps on to Fleet and shouts, "The fox is dead, the fox is dead!" Fleet catches her
and runs into the wood.

"A crow is good food," he thinks.

"Now," Fleet says to the crow, "this is the end. You're my dinner."

30   "That's all right," the crow says.

"Aren't you afraid?" Fleet asks. "No," says the crow. "You can eat me. I'm not afraid of that. But
I am afraid of high rocks."

"That's a good idea," thinks Fleet. He runs through the woods and comes to the high rocks.

"Are you afraid now?" he asks.

35   "Oh yes," says the crow. "Please, please, eat me!"

"No," says Fleet. And he opens his mouth and throws the crow down from the rock.

The crow falls, but then she flies away and laughs and laughs and laughs.

Fleet is very angry. And very hungry.

That's smart!

1 Talk about the people.

1 She's wearing a hat and ...
2 He's wearing a cap and ...
3 She's ...

2 What's your opinion?

The girl's uniform	is	smart.
The boy's uniform	are	nice.
The trousers		awful.
The skirt		...
The socks		
The hat		

3 What's your opinion?

Was könnten das für Uniformen sein?
Was meint ihr?

Colours

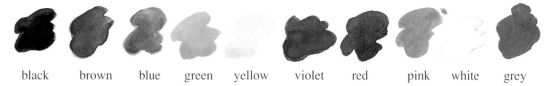

| black | brown | blue | green | yellow | violet | red | pink | white | grey |

4 👥 *Ask and answer.*

coat - jacket - hat - cap - shirt

1 *A:* What colour is the girl's (hat)?
  B: It's ...
2 *A:* What colour is the boy's (jacket)?
  B: It's ...
3 ...

6 👥 *Now you. Play the game.*

A: I can see a (T-shirt).
B: Is it (red)?
A: Yes, it is.
   No, it isn't.
B: Is (Silvia) wearing it?
A: Yes, (she) is.
   No, (she) isn't.

5 👥 *Ask and answer.*

socks - shoes - trousers - jeans

1 *A:* What colour are the (girl's) ...?
  B: They're ...
2 ...

A

Carnival in Paulsgrove

Part 1

Pat: Hello, Kim.
Kim: Oh, hello, Pat.
Pat: Where are you going?
Kim: I'm going to the club. To the Twirlettes group.
    We're in the big carnival parade next Saturday.
    Do you like the Twirlettes?
Pat: No, I don't. I think they're silly.
    Do you like that awful uniform?
Kim: Yes, I do. Anyway, it isn't awful. I think it's nice.
Pat: What about Rick? Does he like it?
Kim: Well, no, he doesn't. He only likes judo.

→ **A1**

Part 2

Photographer:	Excuse me, please.
	Can you tell me the way to the Grove Club?
Pat:	Are you from the newspaper?
Photographer:	That's right.
Pat:	Do you want to photograph the Twirlettes?
Photographer:	Yes, I do.
Pat:	They're silly.
Photographer:	Well, that's your opinion. I like them.
	Their uniform is smart.
	Now, where's the Grove Club, please?
Pat:	It's easy. Go down this road to the traffic lights.
	Cross the road. Then turn left. That's Marsden Road.
Photographer:	Sorry. Marsdown?
Pat:	No, Marsden, M-A-R-S-D-E-N.
Photographer:	Oh, Marsden Road. Okay.
Pat:	The club is on the right.
Photographer:	Thank you.

→ A2

A1 *What's right?*

Kim	likes	judo.
Rick		the Twirlettes.
		the uniform.

A2 *What's right?*

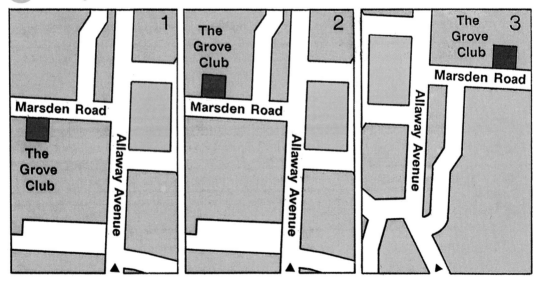

B1 Ask and answer.

1 A: Do you play (tennis)?
   B: Yes, I do.
       No, I don't.
2 A: Do you watch
       (football) on TV?
   B: Yes, I do.
       No, I don't.
3 ...

volleyball *football* *basketball* *squash* ...

B2 Ask and answer.

1 I like Italian food.
      A: I like Italian food.
          Do you like it, too?
      B: Yes, I do./No, I don't.

2 I like sweets.
3 I like fish.
4 I like chocolate.
5 I like Turkish food.
6 ...

B3 Ask and answer.

1 A: Does (Kim) like (chocolate)?
   B: Yes, (she) does.
       No, (she) doesn't.
2 A: Does (John) like (bananas)?
   B: ...
3 ...

	Kim	Pat	Mrs Fielding	John	Len	Grant
chocolate	*				*	*
bananas	*	*			*	*
honey			*	*		
fish and chips	*	*	*		*	
Indian food			*	*	*	

B4 Now you. Talk about your family and friends.

A: Does your   mother   like ...?
                father   play ...?
                sister   watch ...?
                brother
                friend
                ...

B: Yes, he/she ...
    No, he/she ...

basketball *football* *tennis* ...

B5 Now you.

1 A: Do you like (dogs)?
   B: Yes, I do.
       No, I don't.
   A: What about your father/sister/...?
       Does he/she like (dogs)?
   B: Yes, he/she does.
       No, he/she doesn't.

2 ...

dogs *computers* *chocolate* *coffee* *tennis* *Christmas* ...

B6 *Ask and answer.*

A: Do they like (honey)?
B: Yes, they do.
   No, they don't.

B7 *Ask and answer.*

Look at the pictures.

Now ask and answer.

1 A: Can you tell me the way to the club, please?
   B: Go down ..., turn left at ... It's on the ...

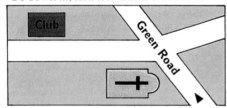

2 A: Can you tell me the way to the cinema, please?
   B: Cross ..., turn ... It's on the ...

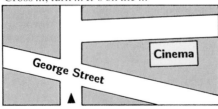

3 A: Can you tell me the way to the sports centre, please?
   B: Go down ..., turn ... at the traffic lights. It's on the ...

4 A: Can you tell me the way to the church, please?
   B: Turn ... at the cinema, ... Green Road, cross ..., turn ... It's on the ...

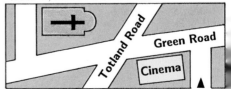

B8 ▮▮ *Now you. Talk about your town.*

Ask your partner the way from your school to the:

1 station
2 swimming pool
3 post office
4 ...

1 *A:* Can you tell me the way to the station?
  B: ...
2 ...

B9 📼 *Listen to the ABC-Song and learn the letters.*

ABC

```
ABCDEFG
HIJKLMNOP
QRSTUV
WXYZ.
```

a [eɪ]	j [dʒeɪ]	s [es]
b [biː]	k [keɪ]	t [tiː]
c [siː]	l [el]	u [juː]
d [diː]	m [em]	v [viː]
e [iː]	n [en]	w ['dʌbljuː]
f [ef]	o [əʊ]	x [eks]
g [dʒiː]	p [piː]	y [waɪ]
h [eɪtʃ]	q [kjuː]	z [zed]
i [aɪ]	r [ɑː]	

B10 *Say the letters.*

1 USA   4 EC
2 GB   5 BBC
3 UK   6 ABC

B11 ▮▮ *Spell the names.*

1 Otfried Bäßler
   A: Otfried Bäßler.
   B: Can you spell that, please?
   A: Yes. B - A-Umlaut - double-S - L - E - R.
   B: Bäßler. Thank you.

2 Your name
3 Your road
4 Your town

(nn = double-n
ß = double-s
ä = a-Umlaut or ae)

B12 *Words: what is Len saying?*

1 Mr Christian is smart.
   He's wearing a blue hat.
2 He's wearing ...
3 ...

B13 📼 *Let's say it.*

[tʃ]
1 Chair, watch, chips, chocolate, French, church.
2 I'm sitting in my chair and watching TV.
3 I'm sitting in my chair and eating chips.

[dʒ]
1 German, jeans, jacket, jar.
2 You can get good jeans and jackets in Portsmouth.
3 John isn't German.

B14 *Make two lists: [tʃ] or [dʒ]?*

chocolate - French - jacket - German - picture - teacher - church - jar

[tʃ]	[dʒ]
change	jeans
...	...
....	

C

1 Fragen mit do/does (Questions with do/does)

Do you like white hats?	*Magst du weiße Hüte?*
Do you like the Twirlettes?	Yes, **I do.**
	No, **I don't.**
Does Rick like the uniform?	Yes, **he does.**
	No, **he doesn't.**

Do	I	like carnivals?	Yes,	I	**do.**	No,	I	**don't.**
	you			you			you	
	we			we			we	
	they			they			they	

Does	he	like carnivals?	Yes,	he	**does.**	No,	he	**doesn't.**
	she			she			she	
	it			it			it	

2 Nach dem Weg fragen

Excuse me, please. Can you tell me the way to the cinema?	*Entschuldigen Sie bitte. Können Sie mir sagen, wie ich zum Kino komme?*
Go down King Street.	*Gehen Sie die Königstraße entlang. (1)*
Cross Station Road.	*Überqueren Sie die Bahnhofstraße. (1)*
Turn right at the club.	*Biegen Sie am Club rechts ab. (1)*
The cinema is **on the left**.	*Das Kino ist auf der linken Seite. (1)*
Turn left at the club.	*Biegen Sie am Club links ab. (2)*
The cinema is **on the right**.	*Das Kino ist auf der rechten Seite. (2)*

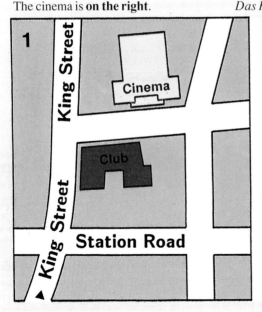

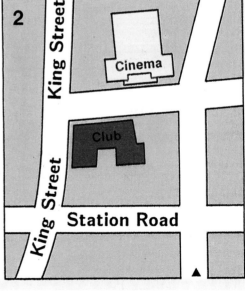

D

18th June

Dear Grandma,

Thank you for the wonderful flowers on my birthday. How are you? We're all fine here. I'm very busy, too. The Paulsgrove Summer Carnival is next Saturday. Do you like carnivals? I do. My Twirlettes group is in the big parade. It's always fun and everybody has a great time. There is a funfair, too, and a lot of stalls with games and food and drink. In the evening there is always a band and everybody dances. It's a wonderful carnival.

Well, that's all for now. It's late and I'm very tired.

Love,
Kim

D1 A letter to grandma

1 Read the letter.

2 Please answer.
a) What day is the carnival?
b) Where is it?
c) Does Kim like carnivals?
d) What can people do in the evening?

D2 A festival in your town

Now write a letter to a friend about a festival in your town. Look at Kim's letter for help.

D3 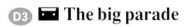 The big parade

1 Listen to the cassette.

2 *In welcher Reihenfolge werden die sechs Straßen und Gebäude genannt?*

a) Allaway Avenue   c) The Green   e) Marsden Road
b) Castle School   d) The Grove Club   f) Service Road

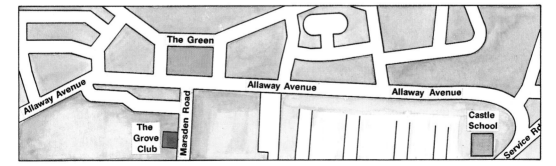

D4 ⁝⁝ Act the scene

1 Ask and answer.

A: Begrüße B.

B: Begrüße A.

A: Frage B, wie man zum Kino kommt.

B: Frage A, ob er/sie die Verkehrsampel sehen kann.

A: Sage, du kannst sie sehen.

B: Sage A, er/sie muss die Straße dort überqueren, dann nach links gehen. Das Kino ist auf der rechten Seite.

A: Bedanke dich und verabschiede dich von B.

B: Verabschiede dich.

2 Now you.

A: Frage B, wie man von der Schule zum/zur ... in deiner Stadt kommt.

B: Erkläre A den Weg.

A: Wiederhole, was B dir sagt.

B: Sage, das ist richtig.	B: Sage, das ist falsch, und wiederhole die Beschreibung.
A: Bedanke dich.	A: Bedanke dich.

❶ The four seasons and the months

Look at the pictures and read the words.

Spring
March
April
May

Summer
June
July
August

Autumn
September
October
November

Winter
December
January
February

❷ 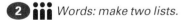 *Words: make two lists.*

1 Schreibe zehn Wörter auf, die dich an den Sommer, und zehn, die dich an den Winter erinnern.

Vielleicht denkst du bei diesen Wörtern an den Sommer:

> *drink swimming green*
> *T-shirt*

Und vielleicht denkst du bei diesen Wörtern an den Winter:

> *white football*
> *television pullover*

2 Jetzt lies deine Listen vor. Wissen deine Mitschüler, welche Liste sich auf den Sommer und welche Liste sich auf den Winter bezieht?

3 The date

Read the numbers.

1st the **first**	11th the eleventh	21st the twenty-first	31st the thirty-first
2nd the **second**	12th the **twelfth**	22nd the twenty-second	
3rd the **third**	13th the thirteenth	23rd the twenty-third	
4th the fourth	14th the fourteenth	24th the twenty-fourth	
5th the **fifth**	15th the fifteenth	25th the twenty-fifth	
6th the sixth	16th the sixteenth	26th the twenty-sixth	
7th the seventh	17th the seventeenth	27th the twenty-seventh	
8th the **eighth**	18th the eighteenth	28th the twenty-eighth	
9th the **ninth**	19th the nineteenth	29th the twenty-ninth	
10th the tenth	20th the **twentieth**	30th the **thirtieth**	

Im Englischen kann man das Datum so schreiben und sagen:

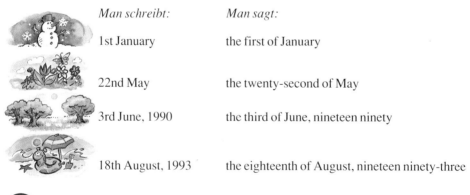

	Man schreibt:	*Man sagt:*
	1st January	the first of January
	22nd May	the twenty-second of May
	3rd June, 1990	the third of June, nineteen ninety
	18th August, 1993	the eighteenth of August, nineteen ninety-three

4 *Say the dates.*

1 3rd June
2 22nd December
3 5th May
4 21st June
5 11th September

6 19th August
7 10th July
8 6th October
9 31st January
10 1st April

5 ⚏ *Complete the Paulsgrove calendar.*

Hier ist Teil A des Paulsgrove-Kalenders. Auf Seite 116 findet dein Partner Teil B. Fragt euren Partner nach seiner Übersicht. So erhaltet ihr den vollständigen Kalender von Paulsgrove.

1 Ask and answer.

A: What date is (Kim's) birthday?
B: (February 8th.)
A: What date …?
B: …

2 Make the complete list. Start like this:

The Paulsgrove calendar
January 19th Mark's birthday
February 8th …
…

A

Ask about:

a) Kim's birthday   d) Madur's birthday
b) John's birthday   e) Grant's garden party
c) Pat's birthday   f) Carnival parade

January	19th	Mark's birthday
February		
March		
April		
May		
June	21st	Grant's birthday
July		
August	2nd	Len's birthday
September	3rd	Rita's birthday
October		
November	11th	Alec's birthday
December	22nd	Grove Club Christmas party

6 *What are the words?*

1 Please complete the words.

a - e - i - o - u

a) y*ll*w   g) b*sk*tb*ll
b) h*mst*r   h) gr**n
c) t*nn*s   i) h**d
d) l*g   j) s*st*r
e) m*lk   k) b**r
f) br*th*r   l) w*t*r

2 What words go together?

a) yellow   –   green
b) hamster   –   …
c) …

7 ⚏ **A secret message**

1 First look at this code.

1	2	3	4	5	6	7	8	9	10
Z	Y	X	W	V	U	T	S	R	Q

11	12	13	14	15	16	17	18	19	20
P	O	N	M	L	K	J	I	H	G

21	22	23	24	25	26
F	E	D	C	B	A

2 Can you read the message?

4 9 18 7 22 STOP

2 12 6 9 STOP 13 26 14

22 STOP 26 13 23 STOP

20 18 5 22 STOP 18 7

STOP 7 12 STOP 7 19 22

STOP 7 22 26 24 19 22

9 STOP

Do it! The first is the winner!

3 Now write your partner an English message in code. Can he/she read it?

1   Inverness

Loch Ness   2

What season is it?

spring - summer - autumn - winter
1   Number one is ...
2   ...

Forest Park, Glenmore   4

Scotland
– the four seasons

3   Edinburgh, Princes Street

The Scottish boy

Part 1

Girl: Alec. We're from the school magazine.
          Can we ask you some questions?
Alec: Yes, of course.
Boy: Well, first, where do you live?
Alec: In King Street.
Boy: Where do you come from originally, Alec?
Alec: From Glasgow in Scotland.
Girl: Where do your mum and dad work?
Alec: Well, my dad works on the ferries to France.
          And my mother is a housewife. But she's looking for a job.
Boy: What do you speak at home? English?
Alec: Yes, of course.
Girl: Not Gaelic?
Alec: Oh, no! My mother knows a few words. You've got funny ideas about the Scots.

→ **A1**

Part 2

Girl: Do you play the bagpipes?
Alec: The bagpipes? No, I don't.
Boy: What about kilts? Have you got a kilt?
Alec: No. But my dad has got a kilt. It's red,
          green and blue.
Boy: When does he wear it?
Alec: Well, he doesn't wear it very often.

Part 3

Girl: What about Portsmouth?
          Do you and your parents like it?
Alec: Well, my mum doesn't like the shops here. And my
          dad doesn't like the pubs. But they like the people, yes.
Boy: And what about you? Do you like school?
Alec: I don't like some teachers. But it's okay.
Boy: What subject do you like best?
Alec: Oh, that's easy. Maths is my favourite subject.
Girl: And one last question, Alec. Do you miss Scotland?
Alec: Yes, sometimes.

→ **A2**

A1 *What's right?*

1 Alec Ross   a) are asking him questions.
2 The boy and girl   b) is a housewife.
3 They work for   c) comes from Glasgow.
4 Alec lives in   d) the school magazine.
5 His dad works on   e) King Street.
6 His mother   f) the ferries to France.

A2 *Here is the magazine story about Alec. What's missing?*

NEW BOY FROM SCOTLAND

Alec Ross ... the new Scottish boy in our school. He ... in King Street. He ... from Glasgow originally. Alec's father ... on the ferries, and his mother ... a housewife. They ... English at home, but his mother ... a few words of Gaelic.

Alec is Scottish but he doesn't ... the bagpipes and he ... got a kilt. His dad ... got a kilt, but he doesn't ... it very often. His mum and dad ... the people in Portsmouth. Alec ... school but he ... all his teachers. His favourite subject is Maths.

B

B1 *What are they saying?*

1 *Alec:*   I like Maths best.
2 *Rita:*   I like ...
3 *Grant:*   ...
4 *Kim:*   ...
5 *John:*   ...
6 *Pat:*   ...

Favourite subjects:

Alec	-	Maths
Rita	-	Drama
Grant	-	Music
Kim	-	Physical Education (P.E.)
John	-	English
Pat	-	Food and Fitness

B2 *Now you.*

A: Where do you go   in the afternoon?
                          on Saturdays?
                          on Sundays?

B: I go to the (sports centre). What about you?
A: ...

B3 *Ask and answer.*

1 *John:*   When do you play (tennis), Kim?
  Kim: ᛫ On (Tuesday).
2 *Pat:*   When do you play (football), Grant?
  Grant: ...
3 *Mark:* ...
  ...

4 *Kim:*   ...
  ...
5 *Alec:*   ...
  ...
6 *Grant:* ...
  ...
7 ...

	MON	TUES	WED	THURS	FRI	SAT	SUN
Kim		Tennis			Basket-ball		
John	Squash		Football				
Pat				Volley-ball	Basket-ball		
Mark		Tennis					Football
Grant		Tennis	Football				Football
Alec	Squash			Volley-ball			

B4 *Now you.*

A: What subject   do you   like best?   *B:*   I   like ...
       When   play (football)?   play ...
       Where   go on Saturday?   go ...

B5 *Ask and answer.*

1 What subject does Alec like best?   – Maths.
2 Where ... he live?   – In King Street.
3 What ... he speak at home?   – English.
4 Where ... his father work?   – On the ferries.
5 When ... his father wear his kilt?   – Not very often.
6 What ... Alec miss sometimes?   – Scotland.

Riddle

What goes 99 tap ~ 1 plonk ...?

A centipede with a wooden leg.

B6 ♟♟ *Ask and answer.*   **Alec's Thursday**

1 A: When does Alec (go to school)?   8.45   –   go to school
   B: At (a quarter to nine).   12.00   –   go home for lunch
2 A: Where does he (go at 3.25)?   12.55   –   go to school again
   B: (He goes home.)   3.25   –   go home
3 A: What does he (do at 5.30)?   4.00   –   do homework
   B: ...   5.00   –   go to the Mountbatten
4 ...   Centre
                                                     5.30   –   play volleyball
                                                     7.30   –   go home
                                                     8.00   –   watch TV/read
                                                     9.00   –   go to bed

B7 ♟♟ *Now you. Ask and answer.*

A: When does your   mother   go to school?   B: He (comes home) (at half past five).
                      father   go to work?   She ...
                      sister   come home?
                      brother go to bed?
                               watch TV?
                               play ...?

B8 *Talk about the people and pets.*

1 **The Twirlettes don't wear red uniforms.**   a) Their house is in Paulsgrove.
2 John and Grant don't visit Len on Sundays.   b) They're Len's pets.
3 Mark and Madur don't go to the judo club.   c) **Their uniform is blue.**
4 Mr and Mrs Ross don't live in Portchester.   d) They like swimming.
5 Mr Christian and Skipper don't go to   e) They go on Saturdays.
   school.

B9 *Talk about the people and pets.*

1 **Madur's father doesn't read**   a) He only speaks English.
   English newspapers.   b) She only likes water.
2 Alec Ross doesn't speak Gaelic.   c) It's always on Thursdays.
3 Len Bignall doesn't go to his club on   d) **He gets an Indian newspaper**
   Saturdays.   **every week.**
4 Madur's brother doesn't sell bananas.   e) He isn't a greengrocer.
5 Skipper doesn't drink tea.

B10 *What's missing?*

don't like - doesn't like

1 Pat ... like monkeys.

2 Kim ... like crows.

3 Mr and Mrs Smith
   ... like hamsters.

4 Alec ... like elephants.

5 Skipper and Mr Christian
   ... like birds.

6 Crows ... like foxes.

7 Mark ... like bears.

B11  *Make a survey.*

1 *Ask your partners:*

   A: Do you like (volleyball)?
   B: Yes, I do.
   C: No, I don't.
   D: ...

volleyball	chocolate	hamsters
tennis	sugar	monkeys
football	honey	elephants
judo	sweets	dogs

2 *Write the answers in a survey.*

3 *Now speak about your group:*

(Five) people like ...
(Two) people don't like ...
One girl likes ...
Only one boy doesn't like ...

B12 *Words: where is it?*

in - on - under

1 It's ... the cupboard.
2 ...

B13 ▄▄ *Let's say it.*

[θ]
1 Can I have **th**ree pounds twenty, please. Oh,
   thank you.
2 Grant Smi**th** has got Ma**th**s at half past **th**ree
   on his bir**th**day.

[ð]
1 **Th**is tea is wi**th** sugar. Let's drink it toge**th**er.
2 Whose bro**th**er is **th**at? **Th**at's my fa**th**er's
   bro**th**er.

B14 *Make two lists: [θ] or [ð]?*

thanks - Maths - with - this - birthday - together -
there - Thursday - that

[θ]	[ð]
three	fa**th**er
...	...

B15 ▄▄ *Let's say it.*

[s]
1 Let's go and **s**ee the ferry.
2 My dad work**s** on the ferry.

[z]
1 She's wearing blue shoe**s** and white trouser**s**.
2 Nice colour**s**!

[s] / [z]
1 Cro**ss** the road now, please.
2 Please, cro**ss** the road now.

B16 *Make two lists: [s] or [z]?*

see - trousers - works - shoes - cross - Scotland -
please

[s]	[z]
bagpipe**s**	colour**s**
...	...

C

1 Fragen mit Fragewörtern und do/does (Questions with question words and do/does)

Where	do	you	live?	*Wo wohnst du?*
What	do	they	speak at home?	*Was sprechen sie zu Hause?*
When	does	your father	wear his kilt?	*Wann trägt dein Vater seinen Kilt?*

2 Verneinung mit don't/doesn't (Negation with don't/doesn't)

I	don't	like	some teachers.		He	doesn't	like	the pubs.
You			the Twirlettes.		She			the shops.
We			carnivals.		It			the fox.
They			robots.					

3 Das ist im Englischen anders:

I **don't** speak French.   *Ich spreche **nicht** Französisch.*

D

D1 ♟ Alec's timetable

Castle School	Monday	Tuesday	Wednesday	Thursday	Friday
8.55			ASSEMBLY		
9.40	Maths	French / German	Maths	Maths	English
10.30			BREAK		
10.50	English	Reading	English	English	P.E. / Music
12.00			LUNCH		
1.05	French / German	Art	Science	Project	Writing
2.15			BREAK		
2.35 – 3.25	R.E. / Music	Food and Fitness	Games	Project	Drama / Computer Studies

P.E. = Physical Education   R.E. = Religious Education

1 Ask and answer.

a) What time is Assembly?
b) What time is the morning break?
c) What time is the afternoon break?
d) What time is (Maths) on (Monday)?
e) What time ...

2 Now you. What's different in your school?

A: We've got ...
B: We haven't got ...
A: ...

3 Write your timetable in English. Ask your teacher for the words.

(D2) ⅈⅈ **An interview**

1 Mache ein Interview mit deinem Partner.

– Zuerst stellst du Fragen an deinen Partner, dann macht er ein Interview mit dir.
– Redet über euch selbst oder spielt bekannte Popstars oder Sportler und denkt euch die Antworten aus.
– Was könnt ihr fragen? Unten findet ihr viele mögliche Fragen. Schaut sie euch an und sucht die Fragen aus, die ihr stellen möchtet.
– Es gibt keine feste Reihenfolge für eure Fragen. Achtet auf die Antworten eures Interviewpartners und stellt die nächste passende Frage.
– Notiert euch die Antworten.

Questions

Do you like	pop music?
	folk music?
	...?
	English?
	Maths?
	... ?
	dogs?
	... ?
	hamburgers?
	tea?
	... ?

Do you play	football?
	basketball?
	...?

| Do you | watch TV? |
| | ...? |

When do you	get up?
	go to school?
	...?

What do you do	in the afternoon?
	on Saturdays?
	...?

Where do you	live?
	go to school?
	do your homework?
	...?

What	music	do you	like?
	films		read?
	sports		watch?
	books		buy?
	...		play?
			...?

Have you got ...?   Can you ...?   ...?

2 Berichte der Klasse anschließend über dein Interview.

(D3) ⅈⅈⅈ **Who's who?**

1 Bringe ein Kinderfoto von dir mit.

2 Schreibe über dich selbst, als ob du eine andere Person wärst:

He/She likes ...
He/She plays ...
He/She lives ...
He/She ... on Saturdays.
...

3 Mischt die Fotos und Texte.

Who's who?

Len's biscuits

Skipper: What's Mr Christian doing now? Oh, it's five o'clock.
He usually makes the tea at five o'clock.
Oh, no, he isn't making the tea today. What's he doing?
He's looking at Len's secret cupboard. Len always closes that cupboard.
Oh! Mr Christian is opening the cupboard.
Where's Len? Oh, it's Thursday. He always goes to his club on Thursdays.
What has Mr Christian got? It's a tin. B-I-S-C-U-I-T-S.
Now he's eating them. My goodness. Len's favourite biscuits. And he's dancing.
He never dances. Oh, good. Now Len is coming.

Len: Mr Christian. What are you doing? You bad, bad monkey. That's my tin. You're eating my biscuits!

Mr Christian: Eeek!

Was man gerade jetzt, in diesem Augenblick oder heute macht, steht in der Verlaufsform (Present Progressive).

What's Mr Christian **doing** *now*?
He's **looking** at Len's secret cupboard.

Was man normalerweise, immer oder regelmäßig macht, steht in der einfachen Gegenwart (Present Simple).

Len isn't here. He *always* **goes** to his club on Thursdays.
Mr Christian *usually* **makes** the tea at five o'clock, but he isn't **making** the tea *today*.

1 *What's missing?*

1 The elephants usually **eat** at twelve o'clock. Today they're **eating** at half past twelve.
2 He usually goes to work at seven o'clock. Today he's ... at half past seven.
3 She usually drinks milk. Today she's ... tea.

4 He usually ... sports on television. Today he's watching a film.
5 She usually comes at half past four, but today she's ... at five o'clock.

2 *Talk about the people and pets.*

1 Mark usually ... with his computer, but today he's ... tennis. (play)
Mark usually plays with his computer, but today he's playing tennis.
2 Grant usually ... on Saturday, but today Rita is ... (babysit)
3 Mr Ross usually ... the car, but today Alec is ... it. (wash)
4 Mr Christian usually ... the tea, but today Len is ... it. (make)
5 They usually ... a uniform, but today they're ... jeans. (wear)
6 We usually ... our homework at seven o'clock, but today we're ... at half past six. (finish)

3 *What's missing?*

1 School ... at five o'clock. (finish)
School finishes at five o'clock.
2 We ... our hamburgers now. (eat)
We're eating our hamburgers now.
3 Listen! Miss Green ... (come)
4 The boys ... football on Sundays. (play)
5 Look! Bighead ... (come)
6 Mr Christian usually ... the tea at five o'clock. (make)
7 Today he ... Len's biscuits. (eat)
8 Look! Madur ... a bird! (help)

4 *Ask and answer.*

1 *A:* It's Monday afternoon. Is Alec playing tennis?
B: Yes, he always plays tennis on Monday afternoons.
2 *A:* It's seven o'clock on Tuesday. Is Alec watching TV?
B: Yes, ...
3 *A:* It's Wednesday afternoon. Is Alec doing his homework?
B: ...
4 *A:* It's Thursday. Is Alec going to the Grove Club?
B: ...
5 *A:* It's Friday evening. Is Alec helping his mother?
B: ...
6 *A:* It's Saturday afternoon. Is Alec helping his dad in the garden?
B: ...
7 *A:* It's two o'clock on Sunday. Is Alec going to the cinema?
B: ...

GHOST HUNTERS

Listen to the cassette. You can act this play in class, too.

The Class Play

GHOST HUNTERS

Grant Smith as *Lord Willis*

Kim Fielding as *Lady Willis*

Alec Ross as *Simon Carstairs*

Pat Miller as *Penny Sands*

Mark Harman as *the Ghost of Willis Hall!*

Scene one

WILLIS HALL
TOURIST HOTEL

Carstairs:	You've got a nice hotel here, Lord Willis. Very, very nice.
Lord Willis:	Thank you, Mr Carstairs.

Carstairs:	So, this is the room, eh?
Lord Willis:	Yes, Mr Carstairs. This is the room. Our ghost room.
Carstairs:	And when can we see the ghost?
Lady Willis:	At twelve o'clock. It always comes at midnight.
Penny Sands:	Is it dangerous, Lord Willis?

Lord Willis:	I don't know, Miss Sands. Maybe it is, maybe it isn't. I never come to this room at midnight.
Carstairs:	It's all right, Penny. I can do judo!
Penny Sands:	Judo? Simon, you can't do judo with ghosts!
Lord Willis:	Now, you must stay in the room and wait till midnight. Take some photos of the ghost when it comes. I've got to have some photos for my hotel brochure.
Penny Sands:	Yes, a hotel with a ghost. Tourists really like ghosts.
Lady Willis:	Yes. We haven't got many tourists but we need them. We need a lot of tourists. We need the money.
Penny Sands:	I see.
Lord Willis:	Now, have you got everything?
Penny Sands:	Yes, Lord Willis. Yes, thank you.
Lord Willis:	The telephone is here. You can phone me for help.
Penny Sands:	Yes, of course.
Lady Willis:	But please, you must take a photo of our ghost. Please!
Carstairs:	Yes, yes. Of course, Lady Willis.
Lord Willis:	Good night, Miss Sands.
Penny Sands:	Good night.
Lord Willis:	Good night, Mr Carstairs.
Carstairs:	Good night, sir. Good night, madam.

Scene two

Eine Uhr tickt laut.

Carstairs:	Well, here we are in the ghost room.
Penny Sands:	Yes. What's the time?
Carstairs:	Twenty to twelve.
Penny Sands:	Is the telephone okay?

Carstairs hebt den Telefonhörer ab.

Carstairs:	Yes, the phone is okay.
Penny Sands:	Have you got the camera?
Carstairs:	Yes, here it is.
Penny Sands:	Look.
Carstairs:	What's that?
Penny Sands:	I've got my cassette-recorder here.
Carstairs:	A cassette-recorder?! Pah. We haven't got time for music. Lord Willis wants some photos of the ghost.
Penny Sands:	Mmm, I know, but ...
Carstairs:	Ah well, let's sit down there and wait.
Penny Sands:	No, let's sit here where the ghost can't see us.
Carstairs:	Good idea.

Scene three

Carstairs pfeift vor sich hin.

Penny Sands:	Simon.
Carstairs:	What?

Carstairs pfeift weiter.

Penny Sands:	Simon, please stop.
Carstairs:	Oh. Sorry.
Carstairs:	What's the time now?
Penny Sands:	Oh, it's twelve o'clock. It's midnight. Brrr!

Eine Uhr schlägt zwölfmal.

Carstairs:	He's late.
Penny Sands:	No, wait! What's that?
Carstairs:	Sssh! Shut up!
Penny Sands:	There he is!

Scene four

Ghost:	Ooooh! Woo-hoooo! I am the ghost of Willis Hall. I walk at night when all men, women and children are sleeping. I am the Willis ghost. Oooh-hooo! Woo-hoo! There. That's my work for this evening. And now I can sleep, too.

Carstairs photographiert das Gespenst.

Carstairs:	I've got it!
Ghost:	What's that? What's happening? Who's there?

Carstairs macht eine zweite Aufnahme.

Carstairs:	There. That's two photos. Thank you, Mr Ghost.
Ghost:	Who are you?
Carstairs:	Simon Carstairs.
Penny Sands:	And I'm Penny Sands. And what's your name, Mr Ghost?
Ghost:	I am Lord Cecil Willis.
	I am the ghost of Willis Hall. I am three hundred and twenty-five years old.
Penny Sands:	Three hundred ...?
Ghost:	... and twenty-five. What have you got there?
Carstairs:	This? It's a camera, Lord Cecil.
Ghost:	Ooh. A "camera", eh? And what can you do with it?
Carstairs:	You can take photos with it.
Ghost:	Photos? Of me?
Carstairs:	Yes. I've got two photos of you.
Ghost:	Hah, hah! Hah! Really! Have you now? What fun!
Carstairs:	Er ... yes. Lord Willis - er the new Lord Willis - has got to have some photos of you. He needs them for his hotel brochure.

Ghost:	Pah, hotels!
Penny Sands:	Yes, tourists like ghosts. And Lord Willis wants the photo because he needs tourists.
Ghost:	Pah! Tourists! Do you like tourists?
Penny Sands:	Well, no, I don't. But Lord Willis needs the money.
Ghost:	Well, I'm sorry. You can't take photos of me.
Carstairs:	But I've got two photos of you here.
Ghost:	No, you haven't. I'm sorry. I'm a ghost. You can't take photos of ghosts.
Carstairs:	No?
Ghost:	No, no, my boy. Look at your photos.
Carstairs:	Oh, Penny. Look. He isn't on this photo.
Penny Sands:	And he isn't on this photo.
Carstairs:	Oh, no!
Ghost:	No, I'm sorry. You see? Your camera doesn't help because you can't take photos of ghosts. Ah, well. Time for bed. Good night, Mr Carstairs.
Carstairs:	Er ...
Ghost:	Good night, Miss Sands. And say hello to Lord Willis when you see him.
Penny Sands:	Yes. Good night, Lord Cecil. 'Night!

Scene five

Carstairs:	Oh dear, Penny. What can we do now? We haven't got the photos. We're terrible ghost hunters.
Penny Sands:	Oh, no, we aren't!
Carstairs:	Huh?
Penny Sands:	We're very good ghost hunters. Listen to this ...

And what's your name, Mr Ghost?

I am Lord Cecil Willis.

I am the ghost of Willis Hall.

I am three hundred and twenty-five years old.

Carstairs:	Hey, Penny! The cassette- recorder! What a great idea!
Penny hebt den Telefonhörer ab und wählt.	
Lord Willis:	Hello.
Penny Sands:	Hello, Lord Willis. This is Penny Sands here. We've got your ghost.

Hier und auf Seite 34 findet ihr zwei sehr ähnliche Bilder. Sie enthalten jedoch acht kleine Unterschiede, die ihr in Partnerarbeit herausfinden könnt. Einer von euch sieht das Bild auf dieser Seite an, der andere schlägt die Seite 34 auf. Fragt eueren Partner nach seinem Bild!

Have you got …?
Has … got …?

Is … in/on …?
I've got … in my picture. What about you?

Zu ❺ **auf Seite 101: Complete the Paulsgrove calendar.**

B

Ask about:

a) Mark's birthday
b) Grant's birthday
c) Len's birthday
d) Rita's birthday
e) Alec's birthday
f) Grove Club Christmas party

January		
February	8th	Kim's birthday
March	21st	John's birthday
April		
May	19th	Pat's birthday
June	22nd	Grant's garden party
July	25th	Carnival parade
August		
September		
October	6th	Madur's birthday
November		
December		

1 People

What a nice friend!

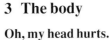

1 baby
2 child
3 girl
4 boy
5 pupil
6 woman
7 lady
8 man
9 partner
10 friend
11 neighbour
12 tourist
13 clown
14 housewife
15 newsagent
16 greengrocer
17 fisherman
18 sailor
19 postman
20 teacher
21 professor

12　**13**

18　**19**

Wow! That's a great ghost!

2 Feelings

How are you?
I'm fine.

1 fine
2 glad
3 happy
4 angry

What's the matter?
It's awful.

1 bad
2 boring
3 silly
4 awful

That's good!

1 nice
2 great
3 wonderful
4 fantastic
5 funny
6 clever

3 The body

Oh, my head hurts.

1 head
2 eye
3 mouth
4 arm
5 hand
6 finger
7 leg
8 foot

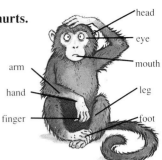

head
eye
mouth
arm
hand
finger
leg
foot

4 Food and drink

I'm hungry!
Well, you can eat bread...

1 bread
2 honey
3 biscuits
4 cakes
5 sugar
6 hamburgers
7 beef
8 fish
9 chips
10 vegetables
11 pies
12 apples
13 bananas
14 sweets
15 chocolate
16 nuts

3

15

SUGAR

5

11

4

2

HON

1

... and you can drink milk...

1 milk
2 water
3 tea
4 coffee

... for breakfast.

1 breakfast
2 lunch
3 teatime
4 dinner

5 Clothes

I'm wearing a shirt and red trousers.

1 cap
2 hat
3 blouse
4 skirt
5 dress
6 coat
7 shirt
8 pullover
9 jacket
10 trousers
11 jeans
12 socks
13 shoes

You're smart!

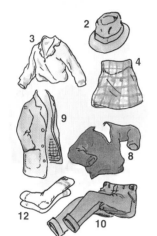

6 The family

This is my cousin.

1 grandmother
2 grandfather
3 mother (mum)
4 father (dad)
5 daughter
6 son
7 sister
8 brother
9 aunt
10 uncle
11 cousin

7 Pets and animals

John doesn't like crows.

1 bird
2 crow
3 hamster
4 dog
5 monkey
6 fox
7 bear
8 elephant

8 In the classroom

There's a rubber.

1 biro
2 pen
3 pencil
4 rubber
5 book
6 chair
7 desk
8 blackboard
9 window
10 door

9 Sports

My favourite sport is volleyball.

1 basketball
2 volleyball
3 football
4 tennis
5 squash
6 judo
7 swimming

10 It's fun!

I like comics.

1 hobby
2 song
3 quiz
4 poster
5 magazine
6 comic
7 camera
8 computer
9 cassette- recorder
10 stereo
11 television
12 video

I'm going to the sports centre.

1 picnic
2 party
3 park
4 game
5 swimming pool
6 sports centre
7 club
8 funfair
9 film
10 cinema
11 festival

11 What are they doing?

She's crossing the road.
They're playing football.

1 sitting
2 standing
3 lying down
4 walking
5 running
6 flying
7 falling
8 eating
9 drinking
10 talking
11 singing
12 reading
13 watching TV
14 babysitting
15 phoning
16 washing the car
17 playing basketball
18 crossing the road
19 shopping
20 selling vegetables

12 Colours

The shoes are green.

1 black
2 brown
3 blue
4 green
5 yellow
6 violet
7 red
8 pink
9 white
10 grey

13 The time of day

1 morning
2 afternoon
3 evening
4 day
5 night

14 The days of the week

Today is Wednesday.

1 Monday
2 Tuesday
3 Wednesday
4 Thursday
5 Friday
6 Saturday
7 Sunday

15 The months and the seasons

It's January.

1 January
2 February
3 March
4 April
5 May
6 June
7 July
8 August
9 September
10 October
11 November
12 December

1 spring
2 summer
3 autumn
4 winter

Grammar

Liebe Schülerin, lieber Schüler!

Auf den folgenden Seiten findest du noch einmal alles gesammelt, was du im ersten Band von ENGLISH LIVE an Grammatik durchnimmst. So kannst du unabhängig von der Unit, die gerade dran ist, alles nachschlagen und eventuell noch einmal lernen. Manches wird dir vielleicht auch klarer, wenn du es in der Übersicht siehst.

Wenn du unsicher mit den grammatischen Bezeichnungen bist, kannst du in der unten stehenden Tabelle nachsehen, wie die deutschen Bezeichnungen auf Englisch oder Lateinisch heißen.

Übrigens: Der lustige Coco kann einfach seinen Mund nicht halten und redet immer dazwischen. Aber sieh dir seine Sprüche ruhig genauer an, denn sie sind gar nicht so dumm....

Übersicht der wichtigsten grammatischen Bezeichnungen in Deutsch/Englisch/Lateinisch

1. Laute

Selbstlaut — Vowel/Vokal   (a, e, i, o, u)
Mitlaut — Consonant/Konsonant   (z. B. p, t, k, b, d, g, m, n, l, r)

2. Wortarten

Wie die Wörter heißen:	Wie man die Bildungen der Wörter nennt:
Zeitwort – Verb/Verb Hilfszeitwort – Auxiliary/Hilfsverb	Grundform – Infinitive/Infinitiv Einfache Gegenwart – Present Simple Verlaufsform (-ing-Form) – Present Progressive
Hauptwort – Noun/Nomen Fürwort – Pronoun/Pronomen Persönliches Fürwort – Personal Pronoun/ Personalpronomen Besitzanzeigendes Fürwort – Possessive Pronoun/ Possessivpronomen	Männlich – Masculine/Maskulin Weiblich – Feminine/Feminin Sächlich – Neuter/Neutrum Einzahl – Singular/Singular Mehrzahl – Plural/Plural
Geschlechtswort – Article/Artikel Eigenschaftswort – Adjective/Adjektiv Verhältniswort – Preposition/Präposition	Wer-Fall – Subject Form/Subjektform Wen-, Wem-Fall – Object Form/Objektform Wessen-Fall – Genitive/Genitiv

3. Satz

Wie die Satzglieder heißen:	Welche Wörter in die Satzglieder gehören:
Satzaussage – Predicate/Prädikat	Hilfsverben (be, have, can, do) Verben (go, play usw.)
Satzgegenstand – Subject/Subjekt	Nomen oder Pronomen im Subjektfall und ihre Beiwörter (Adjektive, Artikel)
Objekt – Object/Objekt	Nomen oder Pronomen im Wem-/Wen-Fall und ihre Beiwörter (Adjektiv, Artikel, Präposition)
Objekt-Erweiterung – Adverbial/Adverbiale	Nomen oder Pronomen, nach denen man WIE, WANN, WIE OFT usw. fragt, und ihre Beiwörter
Satzergänzung: So nennt man Objekt und Objekterweiterung zusammen.	

Bereich Verb

1. Auxiliary Verbs / Hilfsverben / Hilfszeitwörter – BE, HAVE, CAN und DO

a) Bildung von BE, HAVE, CAN und DO

be (*sein*)

I	**am**	(I'm)	*ich*	*bin*
you	**are**	(you're)	*du*	*bist/Sie sind*
he	**is**	(he's)	*er*	*ist*
she	**is**	(she's)	*sie*	*ist*
it	**is**	(it's)	*es*	*ist*
we	**are**	(we're)	*wir*	*sind*
you	**are**	(you're)	*ihr*	*seid/Sie sind*
they	**are**	(they're)	*sie*	*sind*

➤ *Unit 1, S. 2, 6, 11, 14, 16*

be und **have** haben auch Kurzformen. Diese findest du vor allem im gesprochenen Englisch, seltener im geschriebenen.

have (got) (*haben*)

I	**have**	(got)	(I've got)	*ich habe*
you	**have**	(got)	(you've got)	*du hast/Sie haben*
he	**has**	(got)	(he's got)	*er hat*
she	**has**	(got)	(she's got)	*sie hat*
it	**has**	(got)	(it's got)	*es hat*
we	**have**	(got)	(we've got)	*wir haben*
you	**have**	(got)	(you've got)	*ihr habt/Sie haben*
they	**have**	(got)	(they've got)	*sie haben*

➤ *Unit 2, S. 22*   ➤ *Unit 3, S. 31*

have in Verbindung mit **got** bedeutet *haben, besitzen*. Bei **have got** bleibt **got** immer gleich.
have wird zu **has** bei **he/she/it**.
(→ Vergleiche auch Nr. 3, S.124)

can (*können, dürfen*)

I	**can**	*ich kann/darf*
you	**can**	*du kannst/darfst*
he	**can**	*er kann/darf*
she	**can**	*sie kann/darf*
it	**can**	*es kann/darf*
we	**can**	*wir können/dürfen*
you	**can**	*ihr könnt/dürft*
they	**can**	*sie können/dürfen*

➤ *Unit 6, S. 60*

do (*tun*)

I	**do**	*ich 'tue'*
you	**do**	*du 'tust'*
he	**does**	*er 'tut'*
she	**does**	*sie 'tut'*
it	**does**	*es 'tut'*
we	**do**	*wir 'tun'*
you	**do**	*ihr 'tut'*
they	**do**	*sie 'tun'*

➤ *Unit 10, S. 96*

can und **do** haben keine Kurzformen.
can verändert sich nie.

do wird zu **does** bei **he/she/it**.
(→ zum **-s** bei **he/she/it** vergleiche auch Nr. 3, S.124)
⚠ Aussprache von **does**: [dʌz].

b) Verneinung von BE, HAVE, CAN und DO: Langform

	be	
I	am	**not**
you	are	**not**
he	is	**not**
she	is	**not**
it	is	**not**
we	are	**not**
you	are	**not**
they	are	**not**

	have got		
	have	**not**	got
	have	**not**	got
	has	**not**	got
	has	not	got
	has	**not**	got
	have	**not**	got
	have	**not**	got
	have	**not**	got

Ich bin nicht....

➤ *Unit 1, S. 16*

Ich habe nicht/kein....

➤ *Unit 3, S. 31*

Um **be**, **have**, **can** und **do** zu verneinen, fügst du nur **not** (*nicht, kein*) hinzu.

	can
I	can**not**
you	can**not**
he	can**not**
she	can**not**
it	can**not**
we	can**not**
you	can**not**
they	can**not**

	do	
I	do	**not**
you	do	**not**
he	does	**not**
she	does	**not**
it	does	**not**
we	do	**not**
you	do	**not**
they	do	**not**

Ich kann nicht....

➤ *Unit 6, S. 60*

Ich tue nicht....

➤ *Unit 10, S. 96*

⚠ Bei **can** schreibt man das **not** mit **can** zu einem Wort zusammen.

c) Verneinung von BE, HAVE, CAN und DO: Kurzform

	be	**have**	**can**	**do**
I	**am not**	have**n't** got	can**'t**	do **n't**
you	are**n't**	have**n't** got	can**'t**	do **n't**
he	is**n't**	has**n't** got	can**'t**	does**n't**
she	is**n't**	has**n't** got	can**'t**	does**n't**
it	is**n't**	has**n't** got	can**'t**	does**n't**
we	are**n't**	have**n't** got	can**'t**	do **n't**
you	are**n't**	have**n't** got	can**'t**	do **n't**
they	are**n't**	have**n't** got	can**'t**	do **n't**

➤ *Unit 1, S. 6, 14, 16* ➤ *Unit 3, S. 31* ➤ *Unit 6, S. 60* ➤ *Unit 10, S. 96*
➤ *Unit 11, S. 108*

not wird zu **n't**. Diese Kurzform wird immer mit der Form von **be**, **have**, **can** und **do** als ein Wort zusammengeschrieben.

⚠ Bei **I am** (**I'm**) kann man das **not** nicht verkürzen.

Bei **can** fällt in der verkürzten Verneinung eins der beiden **-n-** weg.

2. The Present Progressive / Die Verlaufsform der Gegenwart (-ing-Form)

a) Die Bildung des Present Progressive

	be	+	Grundform	ing	
I	am	(I'm)	eat**ing**	a banana.	
You	are	(You're)	help**ing**	me.	
He	is	(He's)	do**ing**	his homework.	
She	is	(She's)	do**ing**	her homework.	
It	is	(It's)	rain**ing**.		*(Es regnet.)*
We	are	(We're)	play**ing**	cards.	
You	are	(You're)	watch**ing**	TV.	
They	are	(they're)	look**ing**	at the house.	

Das Present Progressive
bildest du aus:
1. einer Form von
   be (**am/are/is**);
2. der Grundform des
   Verbs mit einem
   angehängten **-ing**.

➤ *Unit 4, S. 41* ➤ *Unit 5, S. 50*

b) Schreibregeln für das Present Progressive

mak**e** – making
complet**e** – completing
hav**e** – having
com**e** – coming
danc**e** – dancing
giv**e** – giving
liv**e** – living

-e → -eing

Wenn die Grundform ein **-e**
am Ende hat, das man nicht
mitspricht, dann verschwin-
det dieses bei der Bildung
der **ing**-Form.

forget – forge**tt**ing
sit – si**tt**ing
run – ru**nn**ing
sho**p** – sho**pp**ing
stop – sto**pp**ing

-t	→	-tting
-n	→	-nning
-p	→	-pping

Ein einfacher Mitlaut (z.B.
p, t, n) am Ende der Grundform wird bei der **-ing**-Form
verdoppelt, wenn ein Selbstlaut davor steht (**a, e, i, o, u**),
der kurz und betont ist.

➤ *Unit 4, S.41* ➤ *Unit 5, S.50*

c) Die Verneinung des Present Progressive

	be	+ not	+	Grundform	ing	
I	am	**not**	('m **not**)	eat**ing**.		
You	are	**not**	('are**n't**)	help**ing**	me.	
He	is	**not**	('is**n't**)	do**ing**	his homework.	
She	is	**not**	('is**n't**)	do**ing**	her homework.	
It	is	**not**	('is**n't**)	rain**ing**.		
We	are	**not**	('are**n't**)	play**ing**	cards.	
You	are	**not**	('are**n't**)	watch**ing**	TV.	
They	are	**not**	('are**n't**)	look**ing**	at the house.	

Bei der Verneinung tritt **not**
(oder **n't**) zwischen **be**-Form
(**am/is/are**) und **-ing**-Form.

➤ *Unit 5, S. 50*

d) Das Present Progressive in Frage und Antwort

Frage	Kurzantwort: JA	Kurzantwort: NEIN	
Are you washing the vegetables?	Yes, I **am**.	No, I'**m not**.	Bei Kurzantworten ge-
Is he listening?	Yes, he **is**.	No, he **isn't**.	brauchst du nur die bejahte
Is she buying a pen?	Yes, she **is**.	No, she **isn't**.	oder verneinte Form von **be**
Is it raining? *(Regnet es?)*	Yes, it **is**.	No, it **isn't**.	(**am/is/are**).
Are we going to the club?	Yes, we **are**.	No, we **aren't**.	
Are you doing your homework?	Yes, we **are**.	No, we **aren't**.	
Are they helping you?	Yes, they **are**.	No, they **aren't**.	

➤ *Unit 4, S. 41*   ➤ *Unit 5 S. 50*

3. The Present Simple / Das einfache Präsens / Die einfache Gegenwart

Ich wohne in einem Haus.

I	live	
You	live	
He	**lives**	
She	**lives**	in a
It	**lives**	house.
We	live	
You	live	
They	live	

➤ *Unit 7, S. 68*

Ich spreche Englisch.

I	speak	
You	speak	
He	**speaks**	
She	**speaks**	English.
It	**speaks**	
We	speak	
You	speak	
They	speak	

➤ *Unit 9, S. 87*

Für die Bildung des Present Simple musst du dir eins merken:
Bei **he/she/it** wird ein **-s** an die Grundform angehängt.

to wat**ch**	–	he watch**es**
to wa**sh**	–	he wash**es**
to mi**ss**	–	he miss**es**

-ch		Aussprache:
-sh	+ es	[ɪz]
-ss		

Bei manchen Verben kommt noch ein **-e-** zwischen Grundform und **he/she/it -s**:
– wenn die Grundform auf einen Zischlaut (**-ch, -x, -ss, -sh**) endet;
– bei **do** und **go**.

			Aussprache:
to do	–	he do**es**	[dʌz]
to go	–	he go**es**	[gəʊz]

➤ *Unit 8, S. 78*

4. Wie du Present Progressive und einfaches Präsens gebrauchst

Present Simple: I usually **watch** TV on Thursdays.

Das Present Simple verwendest du, wenn man etwas normalerweise, immer oder regelmäßig macht. Deswegen steht bei Häufigkeitsangaben das Present Simple.

Present Progressive: I can't help you now: I'**m** watch**ing** TV.

➤ *Unit 11, S. 110*

Das Present Progressive zeigt an, was sich gerade jetzt, in diesem Augenblick abspielt.

Bereich Nomen

1. The Noun / Das Nomen / Das Hauptwort

a) Singular and Plural / Singular und Plural / Einzahl und Mehrzahl – Bildung und Schreibung

Einzahl	Mehrzahl			
day	days		Aussprache:	Die Mehrzahl bildest du, indem du ein **-s** an die Einzahlform anhängst.
friend	friends		[z]	
girl	girls			
room	rooms			

Einzahlform + s

pump	pumps		Aussprache:
pet	pets		[s]
book	books		

Aussprache:
Nach stimmhaften Lauten stimmhaft. Dies sind alle Selbstlaute (**a, e, i, o, u**) und stimmhafte Mitlaute (**b, d, g, l, m, n, r**).
Nach stimmlosen Lauten stimmlos. Dies sind **p, t, k**.

➤ *Unit 8, S.78*

match	matches	-ch	Aussprache:
box	boxes	-x	[ɪz]
class	classes	-ss ⟩ + - es	
bush	bushes	-sh	
(Busch	*Büsche)*		

Bei einigen Wörtern enden die Einzahlformen auf einen Zischlaut (-ch, -x, -ss, -sh). Bei diesen tritt in der Mehrzahl ein **-e-** vor das **-s**.

hobby	hobbies		Aussprache:
baby	babies	-y → ie + s	[ɪz]
story	stories		

Bei einigen wenigen Wörtern enden die Einzahlformen auf **-y** nach Mitlaut (z.B. **-by**). Hier wird das **-y** in der Mehrzahl zu **ie**. Mit dem Mehrzahl-**s** zusammen heißt es **-ies**.

➤ *Unit 8, S.78*

man	men	*Mann - Männer*	Aussprache: [men]
woman	women	*Frau - Frauen*	['wɪmɪn]
child	children	*Kind - Kinder*	['tʃɪldrən]

Bei einigen ganz wenigen Wörtern wird die Mehrzahl unregelmäßig gebildet. Hierfür gibt es keine Regeln; diese Wörter lernst du einfach.

b) The Genitive-'s / Das Genitiv-'s / Die Besitzform des Hauptwortes

Mr Christian is Len**'s** monkey. – *Mr Christian ist Lens Affe.*
This is Mark**'s** computer. – *Dies ist Marks Computer.*

's

Die Besitzform wird, wie im Deutschen, mit einem **s** gebildet.

⚠ Das **s** wird durch Apostroph vom Wort getrennt: **'s**.

➤ *Unit 4, S.41* ➤ *Unit 8, S. 78*

2. The Article / Der Artikel / Das Geschlechtswort

a) The Indefinite Article / Der unbestimmte Artikel / Das unbestimmte Geschlechtswort

a boy   *ein Junge*
a book   *ein Buch*
a cassette   *eine Cassette*

ein ⟍
       ⟩ a
eine ⟋

Aussprache:
[ə]

Männliche, sächliche und weibliche Formen, wie im Deutschen (*ein, eine*), gibt es im Englischen nicht.

a book   **an arm**
a friend   **an eye**
a blue car   **an Italian boy**
a new stereo   **an old stereo**
a man   **an uncle**

a → an vor   a, e, i, o, u

Aussprache:
[ən]

Vor Wörtern, die mit den Selbstlauten **a, e, i, o, u** anfangen, wird ein **-n** an den unbestimmten Artikel angehängt. Dadurch kannst du Artikel und Wort leichter zusammen aussprechen.

➤ *Unit 2, S.22*

b) The Definite Article / Der bestimmte Artikel / Das bestimmte Geschlechtswort

The banana is good.
The lady is nice.
The car is fantastic!

The bananas are good.
The ladies are nice.
The cars are fantastic!

der
die (Einzahl) ⟍
          ⟩ the
das ⟋

die (Mehrzahl)

Aussprache:
[ðə]

Das Englische hat nur einen einzigen bestimmten Artikel. Männliche, weibliche und sächliche Formen gibt es nicht, ebensowenig eine Unterscheidung zwischen Einzahl und Mehrzahl. Es heißt immer **the**.

➤ *Unit 1, S. 6*   ➤ *Unit 2, S. 22*

the   apple
the   egg
the   ill boy
the   old lady
the   uncle

Aussprache:
[ði:]

Steht **the** vor einem Wort, das mit Selbstlaut (**a, e, i, o, u**) anfängt, spricht man es [ði:] aus.

3. The Adjective / Das Adjektiv / Das Eigenschaftswort

Paulsgrove is a   **new**   part of Portsmouth.
Len is an   **old**   seaman.
Mr Wilson is   **nice**.
My sister is   **awful**!

Das Adjektiv beschreibt eine Person oder Sache näher.

➤ *Unit 2, S. 21*   ➤ *Unit 10, S. 90*

We've got an   **old** house. –   *...ein altes Haus.*
Miss Green is an **old** lady. –   *...eine alte Dame.*
Len is an   **old** man. –   *...ein alter Mann.*

Anders als im Deutschen, haben Adjektive im Englischen immer die gleiche Form.

4. Pronouns / Pronomen / Fürwörter

a) Personal Pronouns / Personalpronomen / Persönliche Fürwörter

Subjektform   Objektform

I	'm ill.	*ich*	Please visit/help	**me.**	*mich/mir*	
You	're ill.	*du*	Pat visits/helps	**you.**	*dich/dir*	
He	's ill.	*er*	John visits/helps	**him.**	*ihn/ihm*	
She	's nice.	*sie*	Kim visits/helps	**her.**	*sie/ihr*	
It	's good.	*es*	We like/help	**it.**	*es/ihm*	
We	're all ill.	*wir*	Please visit/help	**us.**	*uns*	
You	're nice.	*ihr*	Alan visits/helps	**you.**	*euch*	
They	're ill.	*sie*	Grant visits/helps	**them.**	*sie/ihnen*	

Anders als im Deutschen hat das Englische nur eine Form im Objekt.

➤ *Unit 1,*
S. 2, 11, 14, 16

➤ *Unit 7, S. 68*

b) Possessive Pronouns / Possessivpronomen / Besitzanzeigende Fürwörter

männlich, sächlich / weiblich:

(I)	**my**	dad/mum	*mein Vater / meine Mutter*
(you)	**your**	pen/stereo	*dein Füller / deine Stereoanlage*
(he)	**his**	friend/sister	*sein Freund / seine Schwester*
(she)	**her**	name/class	*ihr Name / ihre Klasse*
(it)	**its**	eye /colour	*sein Auge / seine Farbe*
(we)	**our**	car/school	*unser Auto / unsere Schule*
(you)	**your**	computer/mum	*euer Computer / eure Mutter*
(they)	**their**	house/class	*ihr Haus / ihre Klasse*

Das Possessivpronomen hat keine Unterscheidung zwischen männlich, sächlich und weiblich, oder Einzahl und Mehrzahl, wie im Deutschen.

Mehrzahl:

my	sisters	*meine Schwestern*
your	friends	*deine Freunde*
her	brothers	*ihre Brüder*
its	colours	*seine Farben*
our	cars	*unsere Autos*
your	computer games	*eure Computer-Spiele*
their	houses	*ihre Häuser*

➤ *Unit 1, S. 2, 11*   ➤ *Unit 3, S. 31*

⚠ Verwechsle nie das Possessivpronomen **its** mit der verkürzten Form **it's** aus **it is** oder **it has**!!! (vergleiche Verbteil: Nr.1(a), S.121)

Its colour is green.	–	***Seine** Farbe ist grün.*
It's got a green colour.	–	***Es hat** eine grüne Farbe.*
It's green.	–	***Es ist** grün.*

c) Demonstrative Pronouns / Demonstrativpronomen / Hinweisende Fürwörter

THAT   **That** isn't my bike.

THIS   **This** is my bike.

Der Unterschied zwischen **this** und **that** liegt in der Entfernung, die du zu dem Gegenstand hast, auf den du hinweist.

➤ *Unit1, S.4,6*

5. Prepositions / Präpositionen / Verhältniswörter

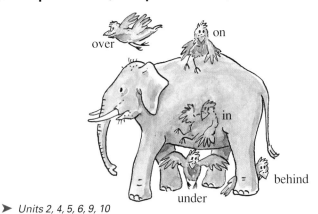

over

on

in

under

behind

Die Präpositionen **on, under, in, behind, over** antworten auf die Frage *WO* ? . Deshalb nennt man sie auch Präpositionen des Ortes.

➤ *Units 2, 4, 5, 6, 9, 10*

Die Wortfolge im Satz

1. Die einfache Aussage

Silvia	*spielt*	*Volleyball.*
Der neue Schüler	*geht*	*in den Judo-Club.*

Silvia	plays	volleyball.
The new pupil	goes	to the judo club.
I	am	in class 5 E.
Grant	is eating	a banana.
You	can have	my bike.
The judo club	is	at the sports centre.

Die Grund-Reihenfolge der Satzglieder im Englischen ist:

Subjekt – Prädikat – Objekt.

Subjekt	**P**rädikat	**O**bjekt
Wer? Was?	Was **tut/macht** …?	**Wen? Was?**

S – P – O macht mich froh!

➤ *Unit 1, ff.*

2. Der verneinte Satz

a) Verneinte Sätze mit BE

Ich	*bin*	*nicht*	*in Klasse 5E.*
I	am	**not**	in class 5E.
Mr Christian	is	**not**	Grant's monkey.

(I'm not in class 5E.)
(Mr Christian isn't Grant's monkey.)

Subjekt	BE (am/is/are)	NOT	Satzergänzung

Verneinte Sätze mit **be** haben die gleiche Wortfolge wie im Deutschen: Das **not** (**n't**) steht hinter der **be**-Form (**am/is/are**).

(→Vergleiche auch Nr. 3(b) und 3(c), S.130)

➤ *Unit 1, S. 6, 14*

b) Verneinte Sätze mit CAN und HAVE

Du	*kannst mein Rad*		*nicht*	*haben.*
You	can**not**		have	my bike.
I	have	**not**	got	a computer.

(You can't have my bike.)
(I haven't got a computer.)

Subjekt	Prädikat 1. Teil (Hilfsverb)	NOT	Prädikat 2. Teil (Verb)	Satz-ergänzung

In einem verneinten Satz mit **have (got)** und **can** steht **not** zwischen dem ersten und dem zweiten Teil des Prädikats.

(→Vergleiche auch Nr. 3(b) und 3(c))

➤ *Unit 3, S. 31* ➤*Unit 6, S. 60*

c) Verneinte Sätze o h n e BE, HAVE und CAN

Grant	*isst*	*keine*		*Bananen.*
Grant	**does**	not	eat	bananas.
Silvia	**does**	not	play	volleyball.
We	**do**	not	like	computers.

(Grant doesn't eat bananas.)
(Silvia doesn't play volleyball.)

Subjekt	Prädikat 1. Teil (DO)	NOT	Prädikat 2. Teil (Verb)	Satz-ergänzung

Enthält das Prädikat keine Form von **be**, **can**, **have**, dann fügst du statt dessen **do/does** ein.

➤ *Unit 11, S. 108*

3. Der Fragesatz

a) Fragesätze mit BE

Prädikat (=BE)	Subjekt	Satzergänzung
Bist	*du*	*der neue Schüler?*
Are	you	the new pupil?
Is	Grant	Len's friend?

In Fragen steht die **be**-Form (**am/is/are**) am Satzanfang, vor dem Subjekt.

➤ *Unit 1, S. 2, 3, 14, 16*

b) Fragesätze mit CAN und HAVE

Prädikat 1. Teil (= CAN, HAVE)	Subjekt	Prädikat 2. Teil (=Verb)	Satzergänzung
Kann	*ich*	*in den Club*	*gehen?*
Can	I	go	to the club?
Have	you	got	a computer?

Auch **can** und **have** stehen vor dem Subjekt. Der zweite Teil des Prädikats (Verb) steht zwischen Subjekt und Satzergänzung.

➤ *Unit 2, S. 22*   ➤ *Unit 3, S. 31*
➤ *Unit 6, S. 60*

Frage nie ohne can, have, do und be!

c) Fragesätze o h n e BE, CAN und HAVE

Does	Grant	eat	bananas?
Does	Silvia	play	volleyball?
Do	you	like	your new teacher?

➤ *Unit 10, S. 96*

Ist im Satz keine Form von **be**, **can** oder **have** vorhanden, so musst du als Ersatz das Hilfsverb **do/does** voranstellen.

⚠ Wenn man **does** hat (**he/she/it**), darf das Verb kein **-s** haben!

d) Fragesätze mit Fragepronomen

Die Fragepronomen
Who, What, Where, When
fragen nach:

Who	is	the small girl?		
What	have	you	got	in your bag?
Where	can	I	sit down?	
When	is	it?		

WER?	– **Person**
WAS?	– **Sache**
WO?	– **Ort**
WANN?	– **Zeit**.

Frage-wort	Prädikat 1. Teil		Prädikat 2. Teil	

➤ *Unit 1, S. 2, 6, 8* ➤   *Unit 7, S. 70*

Das Fragewort steht, wie im Deutschen, am Satzanfang. Gleich darauf folgen die Formen von **be**, **have** oder **can**.

Where	do	they	live?
What	do	they	eat?
When	does	Len	work	in his garden?

Frage-wort	Prädikat 1. Teil		Prädikat 2. Teil	

➤   *Unit 11, S. 108*

Auch hier gilt: Wenn es keine Form von **be**, **can** oder **have** im Satz gibt, musst du als Ersatz das Verb **do/does** einfügen.

What colour	has	it got?	*Welche Farbe...?*
What films	do	you like?	*Welche Filme...?*

Das Fragepronomen **What** kannst du in Verbindung mit einem Nomen verwenden. Es bedeutet dann: *welche*.

How	much	is this?	*Wie viel...?*
How	many	have you got?	*Wie viele...?*
How	old	is your sister?	*Wie alt...?*

➤ *Unit 3, S. 31* ➤ *Unit 9, S. 87*

Das Fragepronomen **How** steht häufig zusammen mit einem Adjektiv und bedeutet dasselbe wie im Deutschen: *wie* und wird genauso verwendet.

4. Sätze mit Häufigkeits- und Zeitangaben

a) Sätze mit Häufigkeitsangaben mit BE, CAN und HAVE

Grant and John	**are**	**always**		at Len's house.
Len	**is**	**often**		in the garden.
I	**can**	**sometimes**	watch	TV in his house.

Subjekt	Prädikat 1.Teil (Hilfsverb)	Häufig-keits-angabe	Prädikat 2.Teil (Verb)	Satzergänzung

Häufigkeitsangaben wie **often**, **always** usw. stehen zwischen der Form von **be**, **can**, **have** und dem Verb oder der Satzerweiterung.

➤ *Unit 8, S. 78*

b) Sätze mit Häufigkeitsangaben o h n e BE, CAN und HAVE

Len	**often**	**watches**	TV.
John	**always**	**plays**	squash.
Kim	**sometimes**	**goes**	to the Club.

| Subjekt | Häufig-keits-angabe | Prädikat (Verb) | Satzergänzung |

Bei Sätzen ohne Formen von **be**, **can**, **have** stehen die Häufigkeitsangaben vor dem Verb.

➤ *Unit 8, S. 78*

c) Sätze mit Zeitangaben

| Len | watches | TV | every **evening**. |
| Kim | plays | squash | on **Thursdays**. |

| Subjekt | Prädikat | Objekt | Zeitangaben |
| | | – Satzergänzung – |

Zeitangaben (**evening**, **Thursday** usw.) stehen am Ende des Satzes.

➤ *Unit 8, S. 78*

d) Sätze mit Zeit- und Ortsangaben

| Len | works | in his garden | every **afternoon**. |
| The boys | are | in Len's house | every **day**. |

Subjekt	Prädikat	Orts-angabe	Zeitangabe
		– Satzergänzung –
		Wo?	**Wann? Wie oft?**

Bei Sätzen mit Orts- und Häufigkeits- oder Zeitangaben gibt es eine wichtige Regel:

Ort steht vor Zeit!

➤ *Unit 8, S. 78*

Hier findest du ein Verzeichnis aller englischen Wörter und Wendungen, die du in diesem Schuljahr lernst. Die Vokabeln erscheinen in derselben Reihenfolge, wie sie vorne im Buch vorkommen.

In der linken Spalte steht jeweils das englische Wort oder die Wendung und dahinter in eckigen Klammern die Aussprache. – Die Aussprachezeichen lernst du in den *Let's-say-it*-Übungen der einzelnen Units. In der mittleren Spalte findest du die deutsche Entsprechung, und in der rechten Spalte stehen weitere Sätze, in denen die wichtigen Wörter im Zusammenhang verwendet werden.

Die **fett gedruckten** Wörter und Wendungen musst du im Gespräch verwenden können. Sie müssen deshalb sehr sorgfältig gelernt werden. Die Wörter im Normaldruck sollst du auf jeden Fall wieder erkennen und verstehen. *Schräg gedruckte* Wörter brauchst du nicht extra zu lernen, da sie nur momentan wichtig sind. Damit du aber auch hier die richtige Aussprache und Bedeutung kennen lernst, haben wir sie ebenfalls aufgenommen.

Aber wie lernt man eigentlich Wörter?

Manche Leute behaupten, man bräuchte sich das Buch nur abends unter das Kopfkissen zu legen. Wir halten diese Methode für sehr unsicher. Versuche es doch einfach mal so:

1 Schaue dir das englische Wort einige Sekunden lang an.
2 Schließe dann die Augen und versuche, dich zu erinnern, wer dieses Wort sagte und bei welcher Gelegenheit das war.
3 Schaue dir das Wort erneut an und sprich es dir dreimal laut vor.
4 Schreibe besonders schwierige Wörter zusätzlich auf einen Zettel.
5 Versuche nun, auf die deutsche Entsprechung zu kommen. Wenn du unsicher bist, schaue einfach in der mittleren Spalte nach.
6 In der rechten Spalte siehst du dann, wie man die wichtigen Wörter im Satzzusammenhang verwendet.

Wir wünschen dir viel Erfolg beim Wörter lernen!

Unit 1

unit ['juːnɪt]	*die* Lektion	
new [njuː]	neu	
friend [frend]	*der* Freund, *die* Freundin	
English ['ɪŋglɪʃ]	englisch(e, er, es)	
word [wɜːd]	*das* Wort	
camping ['kæmpɪŋ]	*das* Zelten, *das* Campen	
film [fɪlm]	*der* Film	
farm [fɑːm]	*die* Farm, *der* Bauernhof	
shop [ʃɒp]	*der* Laden, *das* Geschäft	
sound [saʊnd]	*der* Laut, *der* Klang	
sport [spɔːt]	*der* Sport	
to start [stɑːt]	anfangen	
to stop [stɒp]	aufhören	**Stop!**
team [tiːm]	*die* Mannschaft, *das* Team	
to test [test]	prüfen, testen	

Step 1

step [step]	*der* Schritt	
hello! [həˈləʊ]	hallo!, guten Tag!	**Hello**, Pat!
Pat [pæt]	*Vorname*	

Alec [ˈælɪk]	*Vorname*	
what? [wɒt]	was?	
what's? [wɒts]	was ist?	
your [jɔː]	dein(e), Ihr(e)	
name [neɪm]	*der* Name	
what's your name? [ˌwɒts jɔː ˈneɪm]	wie ist dein/Ihr Name?, wie heißt du?, wie heißen Sie?	**What's your name?** – Alec!
and [ænd]	und	**And** what's your name?
I [aɪ]	ich	
I'm [aɪm]	ich bin	**I'm** Pat.
now [naʊ]	jetzt	**Now** you.
you [juː]	du, Sie	
Peter [ˈpiːtə]	*Vorname*	
Silvia [ˈsɪlvɪə]	*Vorname*	

Step 2

good [ɡʊd]	gut	
morning [ˈmɔːnɪŋ]	*der* Morgen	
good morning! [ɡʊd ˈmɔːnɪŋ]	guten Morgen!	**Good morning**, Alec!
Mr [ˈmɪstə]	Herr (*Anrede*)	Good morning, **Mr** Wilson.
Wilson [ˈwɪlsən]	*Familienname*	
my [maɪ]	mein(e)	
my name is [maɪ ˈneɪm ɪz]	mein Name ist, ich heiße	**My name is** Silvia.
George [dʒɔːdʒ]	*Vorname*	
Miss [mɪs]	Fräulein (*Anrede*)	I'm **Miss** Green.
Green [ɡriːn]	*Familienname*	
Jane [dʒeɪn]	*Vorname*	
you [juː]	du, Sie, ihr	
you are [jʊ ˈɑː]	du bist, Sie sind	**You are** my friend.
Ann [æn]	*Vorname*	
Dean [diːn]	*Familienname*	
Mrs [ˈmɪsɪz]	Frau (*Anrede für verheiratete Frauen*)	Hello, I'm **Mrs** Dean.
yes [jes]	ja	
I am [aɪˌˈæm]	ich bin	Are you Ann Dean? – Yes, **I am**.

Step 3

oh! [əʊ]	so!, ach!	
Grant [ɡrɑːnt]	*Vorname*	
no [nəʊ]	nein	
not [nɒt]	nicht	
I'm not English [aɪm ˌnɒt ˈɪŋglɪʃ]	ich bin kein Engländer/keine Engländerin	Are you English? – No, **I'm not English**.
Scottish [ˈskɒtɪʃ]	*der* Schotte, *die* Schottin; schottisch(e, er, es)	I'm **Scottish**.
American [əˈmerɪkən]	*der* Amerikaner, *die* Amerikanerin; amerikanisch(e, er, es)	You're **American**.
Turkish [ˈtɜːkɪʃ]	*der* Türke, *die* Türkin; türkisch(e, er, es)	Alec is not **Turkish**.
Italian [ɪˈtæljən]	*der* Italiener, *die* Italienerin; italienisch(e, er, es)	Are you **Italian**?

German [ˈdʒɜːmən]	*der* Deutsche, *die* Deutsche; deutsch(e, er, es)	I'm **German**.
Greek [griːk]	*der* Grieche, *die* Griechin; griechisch(e, er, es)	Pat is not **Greek**.
to ask [ɑːsk]	fragen	**Ask** Peter!
to answer [ˈɑːnsə]	antworten	Ask and **answer**!
to say [seɪ]	sagen	
let's say it [lets ˈseɪ‿ɪt]	lass(t) es uns sagen	

Step 4

how? [haʊ]	wie?	
how are you? [haʊ‿ˈɑː‿juː]	wie geht es dir/Ihnen?	**How are you**, Silvia?
I'm fine [aɪm ˈfaɪn]	mir geht es gut/ausgezeichnet	
thanks [θæŋks]	danke	How are you? - I'm fine, **thanks**.
this [ðɪs]	diese(r, s); das	**This** is Alec.
Rita [ˈriːtə]	*Vorname*	
sister [ˈsɪstə]	*die* Schwester	This is my **sister**.
what are they saying? [ˌwɒt‿ɑː ðeɪ ˈseɪɪŋ]	was sagen sie?	
John [dʒɒn]	*Vorname*	
to listen to [ˈlɪsn tə]	hören (auf), zuhören	**Listen to** Pat!
song [sɒŋ]	*das* Lied	
to sing [sɪŋ]	singen	
today [təˈdeɪ]	heute	

Step 5

who? [huː]	wer?	
who's? [huːz]	wer ist?	
that [ðæt]	der, die, das (da); jene(r, s)	Who's **that**?
he [hiː]	er	
he's [hiːz]	er ist	**He's** Scottish.
nice [naɪs]	nett	He's **nice**.
that's [ðæts]	das ist	
she [ʃiː]	sie	
she's [ʃiːz]	sie ist	**She's** German.
the [ðə]	der, die, das	
teacher [ˈtiːtʃə]	*der* Lehrer, *die* Lehrerin	Mrs Dean is the **teacher**.
English teacher [ˈɪŋglɪʃ ˌtiːtʃə]	*der* Englischlehrer, *die* Englischlehrerin	
okay [əʊˈkeɪ]	in Ordnung	The teacher is **okay**.
she isn't [ʃiː ˈɪznt]	sie ist nicht	**She isn't** nice.
awful [ˈɔːfl]	schrecklich	He's **awful**.
to look at [ˈlʊk‿ət]	anschauen, ansehen	**Look at** Alec!
picture [ˈpɪktʃə]	*das* Bild	
in [ɪn]	in	
exercise [ˈeksəsaɪz]	*die* Übung	
right [raɪt]	richtig	That's **right**.
wrong [rɒŋ]	falsch	That's **wrong**.
to talk about [ˈtɔːk‿ə‿baʊt]	sprechen über/von	**Talk about** the film!

people (*Mz**) ['piːpl]   *die* Leute   **People** talk about the French film.

please [pliːz]   bitte

to complete [kəm'pliːt]   vervollständigen, ergänzen

Step 6

in English [ɪn‿'ɪŋglɪʃ]   auf Englisch   What's that **in English**?

boy [bɔɪ]   *der* Junge   Alec is a **boy**.

girl [gɜːl]   *das* Mädchen   Kim is a **girl**.

to come in [kʌm‿'ɪn]   hereinkommen   **Come in,** boys and girls.

please [pliːz]   bitte   Listen to the song, **please**.

to sit down [sɪt‿'daʊn]   sich (hin)setzen   **Sit down,** please.

Kim [kɪm]   *Vorname*

now [naʊ]   also, nun   Look at the picture, **now**.

it [ɪt]   es

it's [ɪts]   es ist   **It's** a nice shop.

a [ə]   ein(e)   Mrs Dean is **a** teacher.

calculator ['kælkjʊleɪtə]   *der* Taschenrechner

to stand up [stænd‿'ʌp]   aufstehen   **Stand up**, now!

book [bʊk]   *das* Buch   The **book** is nice.

pen [pen]   *der* Füllfederhalter, *der* Füller   It's a **pen**.

rubber ['rʌbə]   *der* Radiergummi

chair [tʃeə]   *der* Stuhl   What's that in English, please? - It's a **chair**.

table ['teɪbl]   *der* Tisch   It's a **table**.

pencil ['pensl]   *der* Bleistift

biro ['baɪrəʊ]   *der* Kugelschreiber   It's a **biro**.

school bag ['skuːl bæg]   *die* Schultasche, -mappe   It's my **school bag**.

blackboard ['blækbɔːd]   *die* Tafel

desk [desk]   *der* Schreibtisch   It's my **desk**.

window ['wɪndəʊ]   *das* Fenster   What's 'Fenster' in English? - It's a **window**.

Jim [dʒɪm]   *Vorname*

Andy ['ændɪ]   *Vorname*

classroom ['klɑːsrʊm]   *das* Klassenzimmer

Step 7

Mark [mɑːk]   *Vorname*

classroom ['klɑːsrʊm]   *das* Klassenzimmer   The boys and girls are in the **classroom.**

mum [mʌm]   *die* Mutter, *die* Mutti   Who's that? - That's my **mum**.

Harman ['hɑːmən]   *Familienname*

very ['verɪ]   sehr   My desk is **very** small.

small [smɔːl]   klein   The German teacher is very **small**.

her [hɜː]   ihr(e)   That's **her** book.

his [hɪz]   sein(e)   That's **his** biro.

bag [bæg]   *die* Tasche   The **bag** is very nice.

partner ['pɑːtnə]   *der* Partner, *die* Partnerin   You're my **partner**.

to make [meɪk]   machen   **Make** a list.

list [lɪst]   *die* Liste

you're [jʊə]   du bist   **You're** okay.

* Mz = Mehrzahl

Step 8

sorry! ['sɒrɪ]	Entschuldigung!, Verzeihung!	**Sorry**, Mr Wilson!
dad [dæd]	*der* Vater, *der* Vati	My **dad** is nice.
Ross [rɒs]	*Familienname*	
house [haʊs]	*das* Haus	Our **house** is small.
big [bɪg]	groß	My bag is **big**.
what about . . . ? ['wɒt‿ə͜ˌbaʊt]	was ist mit . . . ?, wie steht es mit . . . ?	**What about** your friend?
here [hɪə]	hier, da	Is your mum **here**?

Step 9

we [wiː]	wir	
we're [wɪə]	wir sind	**We're** Kim and Pat.
Smith [smɪθ]	*Familienname*	
Orville ['ɔːvɪl]	*Vorname*	
Ruth [ruːθ]	*Vorname*	
Alison ['ælɪsn]	*Vorname*	
Stuart ['stjʊət]	*Vorname*	
you [juː]	dir, dich / ihnen, sie / Ihnen, Sie	What about **you**?
we aren't [wiː‿ˈɑːnt]	wir sind nicht/keine	**We aren't** English.
Miller ['mɪlə]	*Familienname*	
Roberts ['rɒbəts]	*Familienname*	

Step 10

they [ðeɪ]	sie *(Mz)*	
they're ['ðeə]	sie sind	**They're** small.
Ramesh ['ræmeʃ]	*Vorname*	
Patel [pə'tel]	*Familienname*	
talk [tɔːk]	*das* Gespräch	

Tasks

task [tɑːsk]	*die* Aufgabe	
quiz [kwɪz]	*das* Quiz	
cassette [kə'set]	*die* Cassette	
clown [klaʊn]	*der* Clown	
professor [prə'fesə]	*der* Professor	
telephone ['telɪfəʊn]	*das* Telefon	That's a **telephone**.
Coco ['kəʊkəʊ]	*Name*	
question ['kwestʃən]	*die* Frage	Answer my **question**, please.
or [ɔː]	oder	
to act [ækt]	darstellen, mimen	
scene [siːn]	*die* Szene	

Unit 2

in [ɪn]	in	We're **in** Portsmouth.
around [ə'raʊnd]	um . . . (herum)	
Portsmouth ['pɔːtsməθ]	*Hafenstadt in Südengland*	
British ['brɪtɪʃ]	britisch(e, er, es); *der* Brite, *die* Britin	

port [pɔːt]	*der* Hafen	
Victory [ˈvɪktərɪ]	*Name eines berühmten Schiffes*	
Paulsgrove [pɔːlsˈɡrəʊv]	*Stadtteil von Portsmouth*	
part [pɑːt]	*der* Teil	Paulsgrove is a **part** of Portsmouth.
of [ɒv, əv]	von	This is a part **of** Portsmouth.
Portchester [ˈpɔːtʃestə]	*Stadt in Südengland*	
Castle [ˈkɑːsl]	*die* Burg, *das* Schloss	
Castle Street [ˈkɑːsl striːt]	*Straßenname*	
West Street [ˈwest striːt]	*Straßenname*	
an [ən]	ein(e)	This is **an** exercise.
old [əʊld]	alt	Portchester is very **old**.
town [taʊn]	*die* Stadt	Portsmouth is a big **town**.
near [nɪə]	in der Nähe von, nahe bei	Portchester is **near** Portsmouth.

A

bighead [ˈbɪɡhed]	*der* Angeber, *die* Angeberin	
at home [æt ˈhəʊm]	zu Hause	My father is **at home**.
room [ruːm, rʊm]	*das* Zimmer	This is my **room**.
I've got [aɪv ˈɡɒt]	ich habe	**I've got** a nice teacher.
computer [kəmˈpjuːtə]	*der* Computer	I've got a **computer**.
have you got? [hæv juː ˈɡɒt]	hast du?	**Have you got** a nice cassette? - No, I haven't.
eight [eɪt]	acht	I've got **eight** friends.
game [ɡeɪm]	*das* Spiel	I've got a computer **game**.
great [ɡreɪt]	großartig	Computers are **great**.
our [ˈaʊə]	unser(e, er, es)	**Our** cassettes are awful.
television [ˈtelɪvɪʒn]	*der* Fernseher	My **television** is new.
we've got [wiːv ˈɡɒt]	wir haben	**We've got** a television.
stereo [ˈsterɪəʊ]	*die* Stereoanlage	Our **stereo** is new.
hundred [ˈhʌndrɪd]	hundert	I've got a **hundred** video cassettes.
video [ˈvɪdɪəʊ]	*das* Video(gerät)	Our **video** is great.
car [kɑː]	*das* Auto	That's an old **car**.
two [tuː]	zwei	I've got **two** school bags.
goodbye! [ɡʊdˈbaɪ]	auf Wiedersehen!	**Goodbye**, Miss Green!
what's missing? [wɒts ˈmɪsɪŋ]	was fehlt?	
to say [seɪ]	sagen	**Say** 'Fernseher' in English!
number [ˈnʌmbə]	*die* Zahl, *die* Nummer	Eight is a **number**.
one [wʌn]	eins	You've got **one** car.
three [θriː]	drei	Have you got **three** rubbers?
four [fɔː]	vier	I've got **four** sisters.
five [faɪv]	fünf	We've got **five** chairs.
six [sɪks]	sechs	You've got **six** biros.
seven [ˈsevn]	sieben	Four and three is **seven**.
nine [naɪn]	neun	We've got **nine** cassettes.
ten [ten]	zehn	I've got **ten** books.
eleven [ɪˈlevn]	elf	**Eleven** is a number.
twelve [twelv]	zwölf	I've got **twelve** pencils.

B

family [ˈfæməlɪ]	*die* Familie	

telephone number [ˈtelɪfəʊn ˌnʌmbə]	*die* Telefonnummer	
together [təˈgeðə]	zusammen, miteinander	

D

again [əˈgen]	noch einmal, wieder	Let's say 'television' **again**, please.
it's your turn [tɜːn]	du bist an der Reihe	
rhyme [raɪm]	*der* Reim, *der* Vers	
to close [kləʊz]	zumachen	**Close** the window, please.
door [dɔː]	*die* Tür	
late [leɪt]	(zu) spät	

Time for revision

time [ˈtaɪm]	*die* Zeit	
for [fɔː]	für	I've got time **for** you.
revision [rɪˈvɪʒn]	*die* Wiederholung	
class [klɑːs]	*die* Klasse	Alec is in our **class**.
Bill [bɪl]	*Vorname*	
to write about [ˈraɪt ə ˌbaʊt]	schreiben über	**Write about** the book.
to take [teɪk]	nehmen	**Take** the book.
piece [piːs]	*das* Stück	
paper [ˈpeɪpə]	*das* Papier	
a piece of paper [ˌpiːs əv ˈpeɪpə]	ein Blatt Papier, ein Zettel	
to stick [stɪk]	anheften, kleben	
photo [ˈfəʊtəʊ]	*das* Foto	
on [ɒn]	auf	The photo is **on** the piece of paper.
mother [ˈmʌðə]	*die* Mutter	My **mother** is German.
father [ˈfɑːðə]	*der* Vater	My **father** is German.
brother [ˈbrʌðə]	*der* Bruder	Bill is my **brother**.
cousin [ˈkʌzn]	*der* Cousin, *der* Vetter	
aunt [ɑːnt]	*die* Tante	
uncle [ˈʌŋkl]	*der* Onkel	
too [tuː]	auch	My aunt is Italian, **too**.

Unit 3

problem [ˈprɒbləm]	*das* Problem	I've got a big **problem**.
oh no! [əʊ ˈnəʊ]	ach du Schande!	
their [ðeə]	ihr(e)	It's **their** pump.
bike [baɪk]	*das* Fahrrad	The boy is on his **bike**.
they've got [ðeɪv ˈgɒt]	sie haben	**They've got** a calculator.
pump [pʌmp]	*die* (Luft)Pumpe	They haven't got a **pump**.

A

Len [len]	*Vorname*	
Bignall [ˈbɪgnəl]	*Familienname*	
hey! [heɪ]	he!, heda!	
you've got [juːv ˈgɒt]	du hast	**You've got** a bike.
flat [flæt]	platt	
tyre [ˈtaɪə]	*der* Reifen	

flat tyre [flæt ˈtaɪə]	*die* Reifenpanne, *der* Platten	
he has got [ˌhiː həz ˈgɒt]	er hat	**He has got** a flat tyre.
he hasn't got [ˌhiː hæznt ˈgɒt]	er hat nicht/kein(e, en)	**He hasn't got** a pump.
Skipper [ˈskɪpə]	*Name*	
to get [get]	holen	**Get** the book, please!
dog [dɒg]	*der* Hund	Skipper is a nice **dog**.
monkey [ˈmʌŋkɪ]	*der* Affe	Mr Christian is a **monkey**.
Mr Christian [ˈkrɪstjən]	*Name*	
how old? [haʊ ˈəʊld]	wie alt?	**How old** is your sister?
teatime [ˈtiːtaɪm]	*die* Teestunde	
tea [tiː]	*der* Tee	**Tea** is good.
cup [kʌp]	*die* Tasse	My mum has got **twelve** cups.
cupboard [ˈkʌbəd]	*der* (Küchen)Schrank	The cups are in the **cupboard**.
how many? [haʊ ˈmenɪ]	wie viele?	**How many** cups are in the cupboard?
milk [mɪlk]	*die* Milch	**Milk** in tea is good.
sugar [ˈʃʊgə]	*der* Zucker	The **sugar** is on the table.
pet [pet]	*das* Haustier	Skipper is a **pet**.
clever [ˈklevə]	klug	Monkeys are **clever**.
man (*Mz:* **men**) [mæn, men]	*der* Mann	Len is an old **man**.

B

handbag [ˈhændbæg]	*die* Handtasche	
club [klʌb]	*der* Club	Paulsgrove has got a video **club**.
riddle [ˈrɪdl]	*das* Rätsel	
giraffe [dʒɪˈrɑːf]	*die* Giraffe	
to pass [pɑːs]	vorbeigehen	

D

concertina [kɒnsəˈtiːnə]	*die* Ziehharmonika	
fisherman [ˈfɪʃəmən]	*der* Fischer	
ship [ʃɪp]	*das* Schiff	
bottle [ˈbɒtl]	*die* Flasche	The **bottle** is on the table.
tin [tɪn]	*die* Büchse, *die* Dose	The tea is in the **tin** on the table.
worm [wɜːm]	*der* Wurm	
sweets (*Mz*) [swiːts]	*die* Süßigkeiten	**Sweets** are nice.
we shall [ʃæl]	wir sollen	
to do [duː]	tun	
with [wɪð]	mit	
sailor [ˈseɪlə]	*der* Matrose, *der* Seemann	
early [ˈɜːlɪ]	früh	
in the morning [ɪn ðə ˈmɔːnɪŋ]	am Morgen	
to rise up [raɪz ˈʌp]	sich aufbäumen	
him [hɪm]	ihn	
till [tɪl]	bis	
traditional [trəˈdɪʃənəl]	traditionell, überliefert	
magazine [mægəˈziːn]	*die* Zeitschrift	The **magazine** is awful.
to read [riːd]	lesen	Let's **read** the school magazine!
article [ˈɑːtɪkl]	*der* Artikel	
thing [θɪŋ]	*das* Ding, *die* Sache	Len has got great **things** in his house.

but [bʌt] aber Grant is English, **but** Alec isn't.
some [sʌm] etwas
help [help] *die* Hilfe

Time for activities

activities (*Mz*) [æk'tɪvətɪz] *die* Aktivitäten, *die* Unternehmungen

picture ['pɪktʃə] *das* Bild The **pictures** are nice.
in the picture [ɪn ðə 'pɪktʃə] auf dem Bild
to play [pleɪ] spielen
pocket ['pɒkɪt] *die* Tasche (*an Kleidungsstücken*)

difference ['dɪfrəns] *der* Unterschied

Unit 4

afternoon [ɑːftə'nuːn] *der* Nachmittag
evening ['iːvnɪŋ] *der* Abend
time [taɪm] *die* Zeit They haven't got **time**.
what's the time? [ˌwɒts ðə 'taɪm] wie viel Uhr ist es? 'What's the time, please?
past [pɑːst] nach It's ten **past** two.
half past seven [ˌhɑːf pɑːst 'sevn] halb acht It's **half past seven**.
it's ... o'clock [ɪts ... ə'klɒk] es ist ... Uhr It's eight o'clock.

A

Madur ['mædʊə] *Vorname*
where? [weə] wo? **Where** is Alec?
where's? [weəz] wo ist?
to do [duː] tun, machen What's he **doing**?
to shop [ʃɒp] einkaufen She's **shopping**.
to buy [baɪ] kaufen She's **buying** sweets.
vegetables (*Mz*) ['vedʒtəblz] *das* Gemüse **Vegetables** are good for you.
to talk to ['tɔːk tə] reden mit Peter is **talking** to Kim.
flower ['flaʊə] *die* Blume Peter is buying **flowers**.
to wash [wɒʃ] waschen I'm **washing** my car.
to help [help] helfen George is **helping** his mother.
bird [bɜːd] *der* Vogel **Birds** are nice.
ill [ɪl] krank Peter is **ill**.
to take [teɪk] bringen
to [tʊ] zu(m) They take the bird **to** Len's house.

to go [gəʊ] gehen She's **going** to the club.
let's go [lets 'tgəʊ] lass(t) uns gehen, gehen wir **Let's** go to school.
woman (*Mz:* **women**) ['wʊmən, 'wɪmɪn] *die* Frau Ann Dean is a **woman**.
to play [pleɪ] spielen He's **playing** with his dog.
with [wɪð] mit Len is in his house **with** his dog and his monkey.

all right [ɔːl 'raɪt] in Ordnung

oh dear! [əʊ ˈdɪə]	ach du meine Güte!, oh je!	
already [ɔːlˈredɪ]	schon	
thank you [ˈθæŋk juː]	danke, danke schön	Say **thank you**, please.
me [miː]	mir, mich	Help **me**, please.
to put [pʊt]	setzen, legen	
basket [ˈbɑːskɪt]	*der* Korb	
Sam [sæm]	*Vorname*	

B

cold [kəʊld]	kalt
warm [wɔːm]	warm
hot [hɒt]	heiß
Mary [ˈmeərɪ]	*Vorname*
Jackson [ˈdʒæksn]	*Familienname*

D

London [ˈlʌndən]	*Hauptstadt von Großbritannien*	
to burn [bɜːn]	brennen	
to fetch [fetʃ]	holen	
fire [ˈfaɪə]	*das* Feuer	
water [ˈwɔːtə]	*das* Wasser	
together [təˈgeðə]	miteinander, zusammen	Let's do this **together**.

Time for activities

to find [faɪnd]	finden	
poster [ˈpəʊstə]	*das* Poster, *das* Plakat	
newspaper [ˈnjuːspeɪpə]	*die* Zeitung	Peter is reading the **newspaper**.
Christmas [ˈkrɪsməs]	Weihnachten	**Christmas** is nice.
card [kɑːd]	*die* Karte	
tree [triː]	*der* Baum	
happy [ˈhæpɪ]	froh	He's very **happy**.
merry [ˈmerɪ]	fröhlich	
year [jɪə]	*das* Jahr	
from [frɒm]	von	The Christmas card is **from** Alec.
Christmas carol [ˈkærəl]	*das* Weihnachtslied	
to wish [wɪʃ]	wünschen	

Unit 5

to sleep [sliːp]	schlafen	He's **sleeping**.
to babysit [ˈbeɪbɪsɪt]	babysitten, Kinder hüten	I'm **babysitting**. It's nice.
to dance [dɑːns]	tanzen	They're **dancing**.
homework [ˈhəʊmwɜːk]	*die* Hausaufgabe(n)	He's doing his **homework**.
to play cards [pleɪ ˈkɑːdz]	Karten spielen	
to watch television [wɒtʃ ˈtelɪvɪʒn]	fernsehen	

A

Friday [ˈfraɪdɪ]	*der* Freitag	
phone call [ˈfəʊn kɔːl]	*der* Telefonanruf, *das* Telefonat	Madur is making a **phone call**.

then [ðen]	dann	What are you doing, **then**?
little ['lɪtl]	klein	
boring ['bɔːrɪŋ]	langweilig	
he's asleep [hiːz‿əˈsliːp]	er schläft	
to watch TV (= *television*) [wɒtʃ tiːˈviː]	fernsehen	Mr Christian is **watching TV**.
to come over [kʌm‿ˈəʊvə]	herüberkommen	
baby ['beɪbɪ]	*das* Baby	
what time? [wɒt 'taɪm]	um wie viel Uhr?, wann?	
elephant ['elɪfənt]	*der* Elefant	**Elephants** are big.
street [striːt]	*die* Straße	Dave is from West **Street**.
in the street [ˌɪn ðə 'striːt]	auf der Straße	The cars are **in** the street.
to guess [ges]	raten	
into ['ɪntʊ]	in . . . (hinein)	The elephants are coming **into** the garden.
garden ['gɑːdn]	*der* Garten	Your **garden** has got nice flowers.
to eat [iːt]	essen, fressen	Alec is **eating** sweets.
to give [gɪv]	geben	**Give** me a chair, please.
them [ðem]	ihnen	They're ill. Please help **them**.
banana [bəˈnɑːnə]	*die* Banane	Elephants eat **bananas**.
apple ['æpl]	*der* Apfel	Give me an **apple**, please.
to forget [fəˈget]	vergessen	

D

birthday ['bɜːθdeɪ]	*der* Geburtstag	Happy **birthday**!
text [tekst]	*der* Text	
to have breakfast [hæv 'brekfəst]	frühstücken	I **have breakfast** at 7 o'clock.
breakfast ['brekfəst]	*das* Frühstück	
present ['preznt]	*das* Geschenk	
to visit ['vɪzɪt]	besuchen	Madur is **visiting** her aunt.
grandmother ['grænmʌðə]	*die* Großmutter	
cake [keɪk]	*der* Kuchen	
cinema ['sɪnəmə]	*das* Kino	Grant is going to the **cinema**.
party ['pɑːtɪ]	*die* Feier, *die* Party	
to go to bed [gəʊ‿tə 'bed]	zu Bett gehen	
Tanja ['tænjə]	*Vorname*	
more [mɔː]	mehr	

Time for revision

daughter ['dɔːtə]	*die* Tochter	
son [sʌn]	*der* Sohn	
comic ['kɒmɪk]	*die* Bildergeschichte, *der* Comic	
Ogg [ɒg]	*Name*	
Yamak ['jæmæk]	*Name*	
like this [laɪk 'ðɪs]	so, auf diese Weise	

Unit 6

fun [fʌn]	*der* Spaß	This game is **fun**.
centre ['sentə]	*das* Zentrum, *das* Center	Ann is going to the sports **centre**.

Mountbatten Centre [maʊntˈbætn ˌsentə]	*Name des Sportzentrums*	
squash [skwɒʃ]	Squash	**Squash** is great.
volleyball [ˈvɒlɪbɔːl]	Volleyball	Peter is playing **volleyball**.
football [ˈfʊtbɔːl]	Fußball	**Football** is a great game.
basketball [ˈbɑːskɪtbɔːl]	Basketball	Let's play **basketball!**
tennis [ˈtenɪs]	Tennis	Silvia is playing **tennis**.
judo [ˈdʒuːdəʊ]	Judo	**Judo** is boring.
free [friː]	kostenlos	
Alexandra Park [ælɪgˈzɑːndrə ˌpɑːk]	*Name eines Parks*	

A

where? [weə]	wohin?	**Where** is he going?
there is [ˈðeərɪz]	es gibt, da ist	**There is** a monkey in the garden.
there's [ðeəz]	es gibt, da ist	Look, **there's** George!
at [æt]	in	There's a club **at** the Mountbatten Centre.
swimming [ˈswɪmɪŋ]	*das* Schwimmen	Alec is going **swimming**.
swimming pool [ˈswɪmɪŋ puːl]	*das* Schwimmbad	There is a **swimming pool** at the club.
what a pity! [ˈpɪtɪ]	wie schade!	
good at [ˈgʊd ˌət]	gut (in)	He's **good at** judo.
all right [ɔːl ˈraɪt]	ganz gut, recht gut	
bad [bæd]	schlecht, schlimm	Sweets are **bad** for you.
not bad at [ˈbæd ˌət]	nicht schlecht in	He's **not bad at** tennis.
can [kæn]	können	I **can** wash the car.
not really [nɒt ˈrɪəlɪ]	eigentlich nicht	Are you good at tennis? - **Not really**.
judo is fun [ˌdʒuːdəʊ ɪs ˈfʌn]	Judo macht Spaß	
idea [aɪˈdɪə]	*die* Idee, *der* Einfall	
us [ʌs]	uns	We're ill. Please help **us**.
I can't [kɑːnt]	ich kann nicht	**I can't** play squash.
a lot of [ə ˈlɒt ˌəv]	viel	
there are [ðeər ˌɑː]	es gibt, da sind	**There are** two swimming pools at the sports centre.
only [ˈəʊnlɪ]	nur	
dangerous [ˈdeɪndʒərəs]	gefährlich	
expensive [ɪkˈspensɪv]	teuer	
well [wel]	also	

B

electrical shop [ɪˌlektrɪkl ˈʃɒp]	*das* Elektrogeschäft	
clock [klɒk]	*die* (Stand-, Wand)Uhr	
to phone [fəʊn]	anrufen, telefonieren	
music [ˈmjuːzɪk]	*die* Musik	They listen to the **music**.
to open [ˈəʊpən]	öffnen	

C

I cannot [aɪ ˈkænnɒt]	ich kann nicht	

D

Rick [rɪk]	*Vorname*	
Peters [ˈpiːtəz]	*Familienname*	
welcome to [ˈwelkəm tə]	willkommen in/im	
fantastic [fænˈtæstɪk]	phantastisch	
bye! [baɪ]	*umgangssprachlich:* wiederse-hen!, tschüs!	
survey [ˈsɜːveɪ]	*die* Umfrage	
group [gruːp]	*die* Gruppe	That's your **group**.

Time for a story

story [ˈstɔːrɪ]	*die* Geschichte	
box [bɒks]	*die* Schachtel, *die* Kiste	
nut [nʌt]	*die* Nuß	
a box of nuts [ə ˌbɒks_əv ˈnʌts]	eine Schachtel Nüsse	
summer [ˈsʌmə]	*der* Sommer	
day [deɪ]	*der* Tag	It's a nice summer **day**.
village [ˈvɪlɪdʒ]	*das* Dorf	
Crickwood [ˈkrɪkwʊd]	*Ortsname*	
the village of Crickwood [ðə ˌvɪlɪdʒ_əv ˈkrɪkwʊd]	*das* Dorf Crickwood	
Mick [mɪk]	*Vorname*	
Pam [pæm]	*Vorname*	
Dave [deɪv]	*Vorname*	
hamster [ˈhæmstə]	*der* Hamster	
Joe [dʒəʊ]	*Vorname*	
wonderful [ˈwʌndəfʊl]	wunderbar	
kitchen [ˈkɪtʃɪn]	*die* Küche	
field [fiːld]	*das* Feld	
in the fields [ɪn ðə ˈfiːldz]	auf den Feldern	
to get into [get_ˈɪntə]	hineinkommen	
let me . . . [ˈlet miː]	lass mich …	
to think [θɪŋk]	nachdenken, überlegen	
key [kiː]	*der* Schlüssel	
always [ˈɔːlweɪz]	immer	You're awful. You're **always** late.
under [ˈʌndə]	unter	
doormat [ˈdɔːmæt]	*der* Fußabstreifer	
lock [lɒk]	*das* Schloss	
to hang [hæŋ]	hängen	
to open [ˈəʊpən]	öffnen, aufmachen	**Open** the door, please.
to run [rʌn]	rennen	
easy [ˈiːzɪ]	einfach	
pond [pɒnd]	*der* Teich	
full [fʊl]	voll	
heavy [ˈhevɪ]	schwer	
tired [ˈtaɪəd]	müde	
to drop [drɒp]	fallen lassen	
grass [grɑːs]	*das* Gras	
hungry [ˈhʌŋgrɪ]	hungrig	
to look for [ˈlʊk fɔː]	suchen nach	

to see [siː]	sehen	I can **see** a monkey in the garden.
quick [kwɪk]	schnell	

Unit 7

robot [ˈrɒbɒt]	*der* Roboter	The **robot** is eating an apple.
to [tʊ]	vor	It's five **to** eight.
a quarter to nine [ˈkwɔːtə tʊ]	Viertel vor *neun*	It's **a quarter to** nine.
to work [wɜːk]	arbeiten	You are **working** and your teacher is **working**, too.

A

super [ˈsuːpə]	super	
to walk [wɔːk]	gehen	The robot can **walk**.
toy [tɔɪ]	*das* Spielzeug	
made in [ˈmeɪd‿ɪn]	hergestellt in	
France [ˈfrɑːns]	Frankreich	
to speak [spiːk]	sprechen	I can **speak** English.
French [frentʃ]	französisch; *der* Franzose, *die* Französin	He speaks **French**.
to live [lɪv]	wohnen, leben	Alec **lives** in London.
to shut up [ʃʌt‿ˈʌp]	ruhig sein, den Mund halten	
a cup of tea [ə ˌkʌp‿əv ˈtiː]	eine Tasse Tee	
bonjour! [bõˈʒuːr]	*Französisch:* guten Tag!	
chemists [ˈkemɪsts]	*die* Drogerie	
Robby [ˈrɒbɪ]	*Vorname*	
Rob [rɒb]	*Familienname*	
fish [fɪʃ]	*der* Fisch	
chips (*Mz*) [tʃɪps]	*die* Pommes frites	
lady [ˈleɪdɪ]	*die* Dame	The **lady** is very nice.
to like [laɪk]	mögen, gern haben	The robot **likes** the lady.
him [hɪm]	ihn	She likes **him**, too.
her [hɜː]	sie	The robot likes **her**.
thirteen [θɜːˈtiːn]	dreizehn	
twenty [ˈtwentɪ]	zwanzig	
twenty-one [twentɪˈwʌn]	einundzwanzig	
thirty [ˈθɜːtɪ]	dreißig	
forty [ˈfɔːtɪ]	vierzig	
fifty [ˈfɪftɪ]	fünfzig	
sixty [ˈsɪkstɪ]	sechzig	
seventy [ˈsevntɪ]	siebzig	
eighty [ˈeɪtɪ]	achtzig	
ninety [ˈnaɪntɪ]	neunzig	
a/one hundred [ˈhʌndrəd]	(ein)hundert	

B

Fielding [ˈfiːldɪŋ]	*Familienname*	
rain [reɪn]	*der* Regen	
umbrella [ʌmˈbrelə]	*der* Regenschirm	
Odd man out [ˌɒd mæn‿ˈaʊt]	*Name eines Spiels (Ein Wort fällt heraus)*	

postman [ˈpəʊstmən]	*der* Postbote, *die* Postbotin; *der* Briefträger, *die* Briefträgerin	
knock [nɒk]	*das* Klopfen	
Carey [ˈkeərɪ]	*Familienname*	
glad [glæd]	froh	

D

letter [ˈletə]	*der* Brief	Peter writes a **letter**.
reader [ˈriːdə]	*der* Leser, *die* Leserin	
Martin [ˈmɑːtɪn]	*Vorname*	
Raffles [ˈræflz]	*Name*	
hobby (*Mz*: hobbies) [ˈhɒbɪ]	*das* Hobby	
school [skuːl]	*die* Schule	Martin is good at **school**.
pupil [ˈpjuːpl]	*der* Schüler, *die* Schülerin	
note [nəʊt]	*die* Notiz	
to tell about [ˈtel‿əˌbaʊt]	erzählen von	**Tell** me **about** your friend.
person [ˈpɜːsn]	*die* Person	

Time for revision

magic [ˈmædʒɪk]	magisch, Zauber-
square [skweə]	*das* Quadrat

Unit 8

neighbour [ˈneɪbə]	*der* Nachbar, *die* Nachbarin

A

every [ˈevrɪ]	jede(r, s)	Len is in his garden **every** after-noon.
to do the shopping [ˌduː ðə ˈʃɒpɪŋ]	Einkäufe machen	He **does** his shopping.
sometimes [ˈsʌmtaɪmz]	manchmal	She **sometimes** does her shopping, too.
often [ˈɒfn]	oft	Mr Christian **often** helps Len.
Thursday [ˈθɜːzdɪ]	Donnerstag	
on Thursdays [ɒn ˈθɜːzdɪz]	donnerstags	She visits her grandmother **on Thursdays**.
week [wiːk]	*die* Woche	
whose? [huːz]	wessen?	
what's the matter? [ˌwɒts ðə ˈmætə]	was ist los?	
funny [ˈfʌnɪ]	komisch	
maybe [ˈmeɪbiː]	vielleicht	
today [təˈdeɪ]	heute	Is it Thursday **today**?
leg [leg]	*das* Bein	Dogs have got four **legs**.
the leg is bad today [bæd]	das Bein ist heute schlimm, es tut besonders weh	
Saturday [ˈsætədɪ]	Sonnabend, Samstag	Today is **Saturday**.
shopping day [ˈʃɒpɪŋ deɪ]	*der* Einkaufstag	
shopping list [ˈʃɒpɪŋ lɪst]	*die* Einkaufsliste	

packet [ˈpækɪt]	*die* Packung	Ann buys a **packet** of tea.
a packet of tea [ə ˌpækɪt‿əv ˈtiː]	eine Packung Tee	
I'd like [aɪd ˈlaɪk]	ich möchte bitte, ich hätte gern	
jar [dʒɑː]	*das* Glas	
coffee [ˈkɒfɪ]	*der* Kaffee	
a jar of coffee [ə ˌdʒɑːr‿əv ˈkɒfɪ]	ein Glas Kaffee	
food [fuːd]	*das* Futter, *die* Nahrung, *die* Lebensmittel	People eat a lot of **food**.
match (*Mz*: matches) [mætʃ, mætʃɪz]	*das* Streichholz, *das* Zündholz	**Matches** are dangerous.
a bag of sugar [ə ˌbæɡ‿əv ˈʃʊɡə]	eine Tüte Zucker	
to learn [lɜːn]	lernen	
body [ˈbɒdɪ]	*der* Körper	
head [hed]	*der* Kopf	Elephants have got big **heads**.
to hurt [hɜːt]	weh tun	
eye [aɪ]	*das* Auge	Dave has got big **eyes**.
mouth [maʊθ]	*der* Mund	His **mouth** is very small.
arm [ɑːm]	*der* Arm	My **arms** hurt today.
hand [hænd]	*die* Hand	My **hands** are big.
finger [ˈfɪŋɡə]	*der* Finger	A hand has got five **fingers**.
foot [fʊt]	*der* Fuß	Peter's **foot** hurts.
Monday [ˈmʌndɪ]	Montag	
Tuesday [ˈtjuːzdɪ]	Dienstag	
Wednesday [ˈwenzdɪ]	Mittwoch	
Sunday [ˈsʌndɪ]	Sonntag	

B

Fuzzy [ˈfʌzɪ]	*Name*

D

bingo [ˈbɪŋɡəʊ]	*Name eines Spiels*
everybody [ˈevrɪbɒdɪ]	jede(r, s)
bed [bed]	*das* Bett
no more [nəʊ mɔː]	keine . . . mehr
biscuit [ˈbɪskɪt]	*der/das* Keks
bread [bred]	*das* Brot

We buy **bread** today.

Time for activities

letter [ˈletə]	*der* Buchstabe	
Ben [ben]	*Vorname*	
to sell [sel]	verkaufen	Mr Harman **sells** computers.
sea [siː]	*das* Meer	
pawn [pɔːn]	*die* Spielfigur	
dice [daɪs]	*der* Würfel	
winner [ˈwɪnə]	*der* Gewinner, *die* Gewinnerin; *der* Sieger, *die* Siegerin	
to go on to [ɡəʊ‿ˈɒn tə]	weitergehen zu	
to go back to [ɡəʊ ˈbæk tə]	zurückgehen zu	
to move [muːv]	ziehen	
to miss [mɪs]	aussetzen	
turn [tɜːn]	*die* Runde	

Unit 9

money ['mʌnɪ]	*das* Geld	We've got a lot of **money**.
coin [kɔɪn]	*die* Münze	
bank note ['bæŋk nəʊt]	*die* Banknote, *der* Geldschein	
pound (£) [paʊnd]	*das* Pfund (*brit. Währung*)	I've only got one **pound**.
penny, pence (*Mz*) (= p) ['penɪ, pens]	*britische Münzeinheit*	
how much is …? [haʊ 'mʌtʃ]	wie viel kostet …?	**How much is** the video?
that's six pounds [ðæts ˌsɪks 'paʊndz]	das kostet/macht sechs Pfund	How much is the book? - **That's six pounds**.

A

really ['rɪəlɪ]	eigentlich, wirklich	She's **really** nice.
cigarette [sɪgə'ret]	*die* Zigarette	
drink [drɪŋk]	*das* Getränk	How much are the **drinks**?
chocolate ['tʃɒklət]	*die* Schokolade	**Chocolate** is very nice!
corner shop [ˌkɔːnə 'ʃɒp]	kleiner Laden an der Ecke, "Tante-Emma-Laden"	
Asian ['eɪʃn]	asiatisch; *der* Asiate, *die* Asiatin	
parents (*Mz*) ['peərənts]	*die* Eltern	Your mother and father are your **parents**.
flat [flæt]	*die* Wohnung	
above [ə'bʌv]	über	
Indian ['ɪndjən]	*der* Inder, *die* Inderin; indisch	
to love [lʌv]	lieben	
Britain ['brɪtn]	Großbritannien	
other ['ʌðə]	andere(r, s)	
things are fine [ˌθɪŋgs_ɑː 'faɪn]	alles läuft gut	
to want [wɒnt]	wollen, wünschen	Skipper **wants** a biscuit.
one day [wʌn 'deɪ]	eines Tages	
all [ɔːl]	alles	
is that all? [ˌɪz ðæt 'ɔːl]	ist das alles?	**Is that all?** - Yes, thanks.
here you are [hɪə juː_'ɑː]	bitte schön	That's £ 6.45. - **Here you are**.

B

I don't know [ˌaɪ dəʊnt 'nəʊ]	ich weiß nicht

D

picnic ['pɪknɪk]	*das* Picknick	
teddy bear ['tedɪ beə]	*der* Teddybär	
wood [wʊd]	*der* Wald	
honey ['hʌnɪ]	*der* Honig	
to match [mætʃ]	kombinieren	
sentence ['sentəns]	*der* Satz	
to go into the greengrocer's [ˌgəʊ_ɪntə ðə 'griːngrəʊsəz]	in den Gemüseladen gehen	
to go into the newsagent's [ˌgəʊ ɪntə ðə 'njuːzeɪdʒənts]	zum Zeitungshändler gehen	
supermarket ['suːpəmɑːkɪt]	*der* Supermarkt	
newsagent ['njuːzeɪdʒənt]	*der* Zeitungshändler	
of course [əv 'kɔːs]	selbstverständlich	

sir [sɜː]	mein Herr (*Anrede*)
greengrocer [ˈgriːngrəʊsə]	der Gemüsehändler
pardon? [ˈpɑːdn]	wie bitte?

Time for a story

crow [krəʊ]	die Krähe
lovely [ˈlʌvlɪ]	wunderschön, herrlich
spring [sprɪŋ]	der Frühling
Fleet [fliːt]	*Name*
fox [fɒks]	der Fuchs
nest [nest]	*das* Nest
up [ʌp]	oben
to shout [ʃaʊt]	rufen
to throw down [θrəʊ ˈdaʊn]	herunterwerfen
to come up [kʌm ˈʌp]	heraufkommen
I'm afraid [əˈfreɪd]	ich habe Angst
also [ˈɔːlsəʊ]	auch
to climb [klaɪm]	klettern
to fly [flaɪ]	fliegen
angry [ˈæŋgrɪ]	ärgerlich
to run away [rʌn ə ˈweɪ]	wegrennen
to lie down [laɪ ˈdaʊn]	sich hinlegen
ground [graʊnd]	der Boden
dead [ded]	tot
fool [fuːl]	der Dummkopf
to laugh [lɑːf]	lachen
plan [plæn]	der Plan
closed [kləʊzd]	geschlossen, zu
still [stɪl]	noch immer
so [səʊ]	also, daher
to jump on to [dʒʌmp ˈɒntuː]	springen auf
to catch [kætʃ]	fangen
end [end]	*das* Ende
dinner [ˈdɪnə]	*das* Abendessen
high [haɪ]	hoch
rock [rɒk]	der Fels
through [θruː]	durch
to fall [fɔːl]	(herunter)fallen

Unit 10

far [fɑː]	fern	
smart [smɑːt]	schick	
coat [kəʊt]	der Mantel	Have you got a smart **coat**?
dress [dres]	das Kleid	Pat has got a nice **dress**.
skirt [skɜːt]	der Rock	Kim's **skirt** is great!
pullover [ˈpʊləʊvə]	der Pullover	
hat [hæt]	der Hut	
T-shirt [ˈtiːʃɜːt]	das T-Shirt	
jeans (*Mz*) [dʒiːnz]	die Jeans	
blouse [blaʊz]	die Bluse	

jacket ['dʒækɪt]   *die* Jacke, *das* Jacket
trousers (*Mz*) ['traʊzəz]   *die* Hose   His **trousers** are smart.
sock [sɒk]   *die* Socke
shoe [ʃuː]   *der* Schuh   Alec has got nice **shoes**.
cap [kæp]   *die* Kappe, *die* Mütze
shirt [ʃɜːt]   *das* Hemd   Peter's **shirt** is new.
to wear [weə]   (*Kleidung*) tragen, anhaben   What are you **wearing** today?
opinion [ə'pɪnjən]   *die* Meinung
uniform ['juːnɪfɔːm]   *die* Uniform
colour ['kʌlə]   *die* Farbe
black [blæk]   schwarz   My trousers are **black**.
brown [braʊn]   braun
blue [bluː]   blau   Alec's socks are **blue**.
green [griːn]   grün   Kim has got **green** shoes.
yellow ['jeləʊ]   gelb   The uniform is **yellow**.
violet ['vaɪələt]   violett
red [red]   rot   Pat has got a **red** dress.
pink [pɪŋk]   pink
white [waɪt]   weiß   The shirt is **white**.
grey [greɪ]   grau
what colour is/are . . . ? ['wɒt   welche Farbe hat/haben . . . ?
   kʌlər‿ɪz/ɑː]

A

carnival ['kɑːnɪvl]   *der* Karneval, *der* Fasching
Twirlettes [twɜː'lets]   *Name einer Mädchengruppe*
parade [pə'reɪd]   *die* Parade, *der* Umzug
next [nekst]   nächste(r, s)
silly ['sɪlɪ]   dumm, albern
anyway ['enɪweɪ]   wie dem auch sei, jedenfalls
photographer [fə'tɒgrəfə]   *der* Fotograf
excuse me [ɪk'skjuːz miː]   entschuldige/entschuldigen Sie,
                                        Verzeihung
way [weɪ]   *der* Weg   Can you tell me the **way**?
Grove Club ['grəʊv ˌklʌb]   *Name eines Clubs*
to photograph ['fəʊtəgrɑːf]   fotografieren
to go down [gəʊ 'daʊn]   hinuntergehen
road [rəʊd]   *die* Straße   The Grove Club is in Marsden
                                                                             Road.
traffic lights (*Mz*) ['træfɪk laɪts] *die* Ampel
to cross [krɒs]   überqueren
Marsden Road [ˌmɑːzdən 'rəʊd]   *Straßenname*
Marsdown ['mɑːzdaʊn]   *Name*
to turn [tɜːn]   abbiegen   **Turn** right here!
right [raɪt]   rechts   Now turn **right**.
left [left]   links   Now turn **left**.
on the left/right [ɒn ðə 'left] auf der linken/rechten Seite   The club is **on the left**.

B

church [tʃɜːtʃ]   *die* Kirche
station [steɪʃn]   *der* Bahnhof
post office ['pəʊst ˌɒfɪs]   *das* Postamt

| to spell [spel] | buchstabieren |
| double ['dʌbl] | doppelt, *hier:* zweimal |

D

grandma ['grænmɑː]	*umgangssprachlich: die* Groß-mutter, *die* Oma
June [dʒuːn]	*der* Juni
busy ['bɪzɪ]	beschäftigt, geschäftig
everybody ['evrɪbɒdɪ]	jeder, alle
to have a great time [ˌhæv_ə greɪt 'taɪm]	sich amüsieren, großen Spaß haben
funfair ['fʌnfeə]	*der* Rummelplatz
stall [stɔːl]	*die* Bude
band [bænd]	*die* Band
festival ['festɪvəl]	*das* Festival, *das* Fest
Allaway Avenue [ˌæləweɪ 'ævənjuː]	*Straßenname*
Castle School ['kɑːsl skuːl]	*Name einer Schule*
The Green [ðə 'griːn]	*Grünfläche*
Service Road ['sɜːvɪs rəʊd]	*Straßenname*
Ocean Radio [ˌəʊʃn 'reɪdɪəʊ]	*Name eines Radiosenders*
before [bɪ'fɔː]	vor
news (*Mz*) [njuːz]	*die* Nachrichten
report [rɪ'pɔːt]	*der* Bericht
Cindy ['sɪndɪ]	*Vorname*
Waits [weɪts]	*Familienname*
to lead [liːd]	anführen
behind [bɪ'haɪnd]	hinter
hill [hɪl]	*der* Hügel
after ['ɑːftə]	nach
to finish ['fɪnɪʃ]	aufhören, zu Ende gehen
to scream [skriːm]	schreien, kreischen
to put on [pʊt_'ɒn]	anziehen

Time for activities

season ['siːzn]	*die* Jahreszeit
month [mʌnθ]	*der* Monat
March [mɑːtʃ]	*der* März
April ['eɪprəl]	*der* April
May [meɪ]	*der* Mai
July [dʒuː'laɪ]	*der* Juli
August ['ɔːgəst]	*der* August
autumn ['ɔːtəm]	*der* Herbst
September [sep'tembə]	*der* September
October [ɒk'təʊbə]	*der* Oktober
November [nəʊ'vembə]	*der* November
winter ['wɪntə]	*der* Winter
December [dɪ'sembə]	*der* Dezember
January ['dʒænjʊərɪ]	*der* Januar
February ['febrʊərɪ]	*der* Februar
date [deɪt]	*das* Datum
first [fɜːst]	erste (r,s)

second ['sekənd]	zweite (r,s)
third [θɜːd]	dritte (r,s)
calendar ['kælɪndə]	*der* Kalender
code [kəʊd]	*die* Geheimschrift
message ['mesɪdʒ]	*die* Botschaft

Unit 11

Scotland ['skɒtlənd]	Schottland
Inverness [ˌɪnvə'nes]	Stadt in Schottland
Loch Ness [lɒk nes]	See in Schottland
Edinburgh ['edɪnbərə]	Hauptstadt von Schottland
Princes Street [prɪn'ses striːt]	Straßenname in Edinburgh
Forest Park ['fɒrɪst pɑːk]	Naturpark
Glenmore [glen'mɔː]	Naturpark in Schottland

A

to ask questions [ɑːsk 'kwestʃənz]	Fragen stellen	
King Street ['kɪŋ striːt]	*Straßenname*	
to come from ['kʌm frəm]	kommen aus/von	
originally [ə'rɪdʒənəlɪ]	ursprünglich	
Glasgow ['glɑːsgəʊ]	*Großstadt in Schottland*	
ferry (*Mz:* ferries) ['ferɪ]	*die* Fähre	
housewife ['haʊswaɪf]	*die* Hausfrau	Alec's mother is a **housewife**.
job [dʒɒb]	*der* Job, *die* Stelle	Ann Dean has got a good **job**.
Gaelic ['gælɪk]	gälisch	
to know [nəʊ]	kennen	Mrs Ross **knows** a few Gaelic words.
a few [ə 'fjuː]	ein paar	
Scots [skɒts]	*die* Schotten	
bagpipes ['bægpaɪps]	*der* Dudelsack	
kilt [kɪlt]	*der* Kilt, *der* Schottenrock	
when? [wen]	wann?	**When** do you have breakfast?
pub [pʌb]	*die* Kneipe, *das* Wirtshaus	
subject ['sʌbdʒɪkt]	*das* Schulfach	
to like best [laɪk 'best]	am liebsten mögen	
Maths [mæθs]	Mathe(matik)	
favourite ['feɪvərɪt]	liebstes, Lieblings-	Maths is my **favourite** subject.
last [lɑːst]	letzte(r, s)	
to miss [mɪs]	vermissen	Do you **miss** Scotland?

B

drama ['drɑːmə]	Drama
Physical Education (= P.E.) [ˌfɪzɪkl_edjʊ'keɪʃn]	Sport, Turnen
fitness ['fɪtnɪs]	Fitness
centipede ['sentɪpiːd]	*der* Tausendfüßler
wooden leg [ˌwʊdn 'leg]	*das* Holzbein
lunch [lʌntʃ]	*das* Mittagessen

timetable ['taɪmteɪbl]	*der* Stundenplan
assembly [ə'semblɪ]	*Versammlung aller Schüler der Schule, Morgengebet*
break [breɪk]	*die* Pause
project ['prɒdʒekt]	*das* Projekt
Art [ɑːt]	Kunst, *der* Kunstunterricht
Science ['saɪəns]	Naturwissenschaften
Religious Education (= R.E.) [rɪˌlɪdʒəs edjʊ'keɪʃn]	*der* Religionsunterricht
Computer Studies [kəm'pjuːtə ˌstʌdɪz]	Informatik
different ['dɪfərənt]	anders
interview ['ɪntəvjuː]	*das* Interview
pop music ['pɒp ˌmjuːzɪk]	
	die Popmusik
folk music ['fəʊk ˌmjuːzɪk]	*die* Folkmusik
hamburger ['hæmbɜːgə]	*der* Hamburger

Time for revision

usually ['juːʒʊəlɪ]	gewöhnlich, meistens	Len **usually** goes to his club on Thursdays.
secret ['siːkrɪt]	geheim	
my goodness! [maɪ 'gʊdnɪs]	ach du meine Güte!, ach du lieber Gott!	
never ['nevə]	nie	
to finish ['fɪnɪʃ]	aufhören	School usually **finishes** at five o'clock.
bad [bæd]	böse	

Unit 12

ghost [gəʊst]	*der* Geist, *das* Gespenst
hunter ['hʌntə]	*der* Jäger
as [æz]	als
Lord [lɔːd]	Lord (*Titel*)
Willis ['wɪlɪs]	*Familienname*
Simon ['saɪmən]	*Vorname*
Carstairs ['kɑːsteəz]	*Familienname*
Penny ['penɪ]	*Vorname*
Sands [sændz]	*Familienname*
hall [hɔːl]	*das* Herrenhaus, *das* Schloss

Scene 1

hotel [həʊ'tel]	*das* Hotel
so [səʊ]	(al)so
midnight ['mɪdnaɪt]	*die* Mitternacht
at midnight [æt 'mɪdnaɪt]	um Mitternacht
must [mʌst]	müssen
to stay [steɪ]	bleiben
to wait [weɪt]	warten

to have got to [hæv ˈgɒt tə]	müssen	
brochure [ˈbrəʊʃə]	*die* Broschüre, *der* Katalog	
tourist [ˈtʊərɪst]	*der* Tourist	A **tourist** usually sleeps in a hotel.
need [niːd]	brauchen	
I see [ˈaɪ‿siː]	(ich) verstehe, ah ja	
night [naɪt]	*die* Nacht	Ghosts usually come in the **night**.
to take a photo [ˌteɪk‿ə ˈfəʊtəʊ]	ein Foto machen	
good night! [gʊd ˈnaɪt]	gute Nacht!	**Good night**, Dave!
madam [ˈmædəm]	gnädige Frau (*Anrede*)	

Scene 2

camera [ˈkæmərə]	*die* Kamera, *der* Fotoapparat
cassette-recorder [kəˈsetrɪˌkɔːdə]	*der* Cassettenrecorder

Scene 4

child (*Mz:* children) [tʃaɪld, ˈtʃɪldrən]	*das* Kind
to happen [ˈhæpən]	passieren
Cecil [ˈsesl]	*Vorname*
because [bɪˈkɒz]	weil
I'm sorry [aɪm ˈsɒrɪ]	es tut mir leid, Verzeihung·
to say hello [seɪ ˈheləʊ]	grüßen, einen Gruß ausrichten
when [wen]	wenn
'night! [naɪt]	*umgangssprachlich:* gute Nacht!

Scene 5

terrible [ˈterəbl]	schrecklich, furchtbar

Wordfields

wordfield [ˈwɜːdfiːld]	*das* Wortfeld
feeling [ˈfiːlɪŋ]	*das* Gefühl
clothes (*Mz*) [kləʊðz]	*die* Kleidung
animal [ˈænɪml]	*das* Tier

Dictionary

Wenn du ein Wort nicht mehr weißt, kannst du es in dieser Übersicht nachschlagen. Du findest hier die englischen Wörter und Wendungen in alphabetischer Reihenfolge.

Neben dem englischen Stichwort, der Aussprache und der deutschen Entsprechung siehst du auch, wo das betreffende englische Wort zum ersten Mal auftritt (Fundstelle im *Schrägdruck*), oder wo es im Zusammenhang erklärt wird (Fundstelle im Normaldruck). Möchtest du mehr über ein Wort wissen, kannst du im Vocabulary an der entsprechenden Stelle nachsehen.

Beim Auffinden der englischen Stichwörter weist die erste Stelle (Ziffer) immer auf die entsprechende Unit hin, die zweite Stelle (Buchstabe) auf den Unitteil, zum Beispiel:

2 I	=	Unit 2, Einleitung (vor Teil A)
4 A	=	Unit 4, Teil A
8 D	=	Unit 8, Teil D

Das T hinter einer Unit bedeutet "Time for ...", zum Beispiel:

| 7 T | = | Unit 7, Time for revision |

Da die Unit 1 und die Unit 12 eine andere Einteilung haben, findest du hier auch etwas andere Buchstaben. Es bedeuten:

1 St 3	=	Unit 1, Step 3
1 T	=	Unit 1, Tasks
12 S 4	=	Unit 12, Scene 4

A

a [ə] ein(e) 1 St 6

above [ə'bʌv] über 9 A

act [ækt] darstellen, mimen 1 T

activities *(Mz)* [æk'tɪvətɪz] *die* Aktivitäten, *die* Unternehmungen 3 T

afraid [ə'freɪd]: **I'm afraid** ich habe Angst 9 T

after ['ɑːftə] nach 10 D

afternoon [ɑːftə'nuːn] *der* Nachmittag 4 I

again [ə'gen] noch einmal, wieder 2 D

all [ɔːl] alles 9 A: **is that all?** ist das alles? 9 A

all right [ɔːl 'raɪt] in Ordnung 4 A; ganz gut, recht gut 6 A

already [ɔːl'redɪ] schon 6 T

always ['ɔːlweɪz] immer 6 T

am [æm]: **I am** ich bin 1 St 2

American [ə'merɪkən] *der* Amerikaner, *die* Amerikanerin; amerikanisch(e, er, es) 1 St 3

an [ən] ein(e) 2 I

and [ænd] und 1 St 1

angry ['æŋgrɪ] ärgerlich 9 T

answer ['ɑːnsə] antworten 1 St 3

anyway ['enɪweɪ] wie dem auch sei, jedenfalls 10 A

apple ['æpl] *der* Apfel 5 A

April ['eɪprəl] *der* April 10 T

are [ɑː]: **we/you/they are** wir sind / du bist / ihr seid / Sie sind, sie sind 1 St 2, 1 St 9, 1 St 10

arm [ɑːm] *der* Arm 8 A

around [ə'raʊnd] um ... (herum) 2 I

Art [ɑːt] Kunst, *der* Kunstunterricht 11 D

article ['ɑːtɪkl] *der* Artikel 3 D

as [æz] als 12 I

Asian ['eɪʃn] asiatisch; *der* Asiate, *die* Asiatin 9 A

ask [ɑːsk] fragen 1 St 3

asleep [ə'sliːp]: **he's asleep** er schläft 5 A

assembly [ə'semblɪ] *Versammlung aller Schüler der Schule, Morgengebet* 11 D

at [æt] in 6 A

August ['ɔːgəst] *der* August 10 T

aunt [ɑːnt] *die* Tante 2 T

autumn ['ɔːtəm] *der* Herbst 10 T

awful ['ɔːfl] schrecklich 1 St 5

B

baby ['beɪbɪ] *das* Baby 5 A

babysit ['beɪbɪsɪt] babysitten, Kinder hüten 5 I

bad [bæd] schlecht, schlimm 6 A; böse 11 T: **not bad at** nicht schlecht in 6 A; **the leg is bad today** das Bein ist heute schlimm, es tut besonders weh 8 A

bag [bæg] *die* Tasche 1 St 7: **a bag of sugar** eine Tüte Zucker 8 A

bagpipes ['bægpaɪps] *der* Dudelsack 11 A

banana [bə'nɑːnə] *die* Banane 5 A

band [bænd] *die* Band 10 D

bank note ['bæŋk nəʊt] *die* Banknote, *der* Geldschein 9 I

basket ['bɑːskɪt] *der* Korb 4 A

basketball ['bɑːskɪtbɔːl] Basketball 6 I

be [biː] sein *(Anhang)*

because [bɪ'kɒz] weil 12 S 4

bed [bed] *das* Bett 8 D

before [bɪ'fɔː] vor 10 D

behind [bɪ'haɪnd] hinter 10 D

big [bɪg] groß 1 St 8

bighead ['bɪghed] *der* Angeber, *die* Angeberin 2 A

bike [baɪk] *das* Fahrrad 3 I

bird [bɜːd] *der* Vogel 4 A

biro ['baɪrəʊ] *der* Kugelschreiber *1 St 6*
birthday ['bɜːθdeɪ] *der* Geburtstag *5 D*
biscuit ['bɪskɪt] *der/das* Keks *8 D*
black [blæk] schwarz *10 I*
blackboard ['blækbɔːd] *die* Tafel *1 St 6*
blouse [blaʊz] *die* Bluse *10 I*
blue [bluː] blau *10 I*
body ['bɒdɪ] *der* Körper *8 A*
bonjour! [bõˈʒuːr] *Französisch:* guten Tag! *7 A*
book [bʊk] *das* Buch *1 St 6*
boring ['bɔːrɪŋ] langweilig *5 A*
bottle ['bɒtl] *die* Flasche *3 D*
box [bɒks] *die* Schachtel; *die* Kiste *6 T*
boy [bɔɪ] *der* Junge *1 St 6*
bread [bred] *das* Brot *8 D*
break [breɪk] *die* Pause *11 D*
breakfast ['brekfəst] *das* Frühstück *5 D*: **have breakfast** frühstücken *5 D*
Britain ['brɪtn] Großbritannien *9 A*
British ['brɪtɪʃ] britisch(e, er, es); *der* Brite, *die* Britin *2 I*
brochure ['brəʊʃə] *die* Broschüre, *der* Katalog *12 S 1*
brother ['brʌðə] *der* Bruder *2 T*
brown [braʊn] braun *10 I*
burn [bɜːn] brennen *4 D*
busy ['bɪzɪ] beschäftigt, geschäftig *10 D*
but [bʌt] aber *3 D*
buy [baɪ] kaufen *4 A*
bye! [baɪ] *umgangssprachlich:* wiedersehen!, tschüs! *6 D*

C

cake [keɪk] *der* Kuchen *5 D*
calculator ['kælkjʊleɪtə] *der* Taschenrechner *1 St 6*
calendar ['kælɪndə] *der* Kalender *10 T*
camera ['kæmərə] *die* Kamera, *der* Fotoapparat *12 S 2*
camping ['kæmpɪŋ] *das* Zelten, *das* Campen *1 I*
can [kæn] können *6 A*: **I can't** ich kann nicht *6 A*; **I cannot** ich kann nicht *6 C*
cap [kæp] *die* Kappe, *die* Mütze *10 I*
car [kɑː] *das* Auto *2 A*
card [kɑːd] *die* Karte *4 T*

carnival ['kɑːnɪvl] *der* Karneval, *der* Fasching *10 A*
cassette [kəˈset] *die* Cassette *1 T*
cassette-recorder [kəˈsetrɪˌkɔːdə] *der* Cassettenrecorder *12 S 2*
Castle ['kɑːsl] *die* Burg, *das* Schloss *2 I*
centre ['sentə] *das* Zentrum, *das* Center *6 I*
chair [tʃeə] *der* Stuhl *1 St 6*
chemists ['kemɪsts] *die* Drogerie *7 A*
child (*Mz:* children) [tʃaɪld, 'tʃɪldrən] *das* Kind *12 S 4*
chips *(Mz)* [tʃɪps] *die* Pommes frites *7 A*
chocolate ['tʃɒklət] *die* Schokolade *9 A*
Christmas ['krɪsməs] Weihnachten *4 T*: **Christmas carol** *das* Weihnachtslied *4 T*
church [tʃɜːtʃ] *die* Kirche *10 B*
cigarette [sɪgəˈret] *die* Zigarette *9 A*
cinema ['sɪnəmə] *das* Kino *5 D*
class [klɑːs] *die* Klasse *2 T*
classroom ['klɑːsrʊm] *das* Klassenzimmer *1 St 7*
clever ['klevə] klug *3 A*
clock [klɒk] (Stand-, Wand)Uhr *6 B*: **it's ... o'clock** es ist ... Uhr *4 I*
close [kləʊz] zumachen *2 D*
clown [klaʊn] *der* Clown *1 T*
club [klʌb] *der* Club *3 B*
coat [kəʊt] *der* Mantel *10 I*
code [kəʊd] *die* Geheimschrift *10 T*
coffee ['kɒfɪ] *der* Kaffee *8 A*: **a jar of coffee** ein Glas Kaffee *8 A*
coin [kɔɪn] *die* Münze *9 I*
cold [kəʊld] kalt *4 B*
colour ['kʌlə] *die* Farbe *10 I*: **what colour is/are ... ?** welche Farbe hat/haben ... ? *10 I*
come from ['kʌm frəm] kommen aus/von *11 A*
come in [kʌmˈɪn] hereinkommen *1 St 6*
come over [kʌmˈəʊvə] herüberkommen *5 A*
comic ['kɒmɪk] *die* Bildergeschichte, *der* Comic *5 T*
complete [kəmˈpliːt] vervollständigen, ergänzen *1 St 5*

computer [kəmˈpjuːtə] *der* Computer *2 A*
Computer Studies [kəmˈpjuːtə ˌstʌdɪz] Informatik *11 D*
concertina [kɒnsəˈtiːnə] *die* Ziehharmonika *3 D*
corner shop [ˌkɔːnə ˈʃɒp] kleiner Laden an der Ecke, "Tante-Emma-Laden" *9 A*
cousin ['kʌzn] *der* Cousin, *der* Vetter *2 T*
cross [krɒs] überqueren *10 A*
crow [krəʊ] *die* Krähe *9 T*
cup [kʌp] *die* Tasse *3 A*: **a cup of tea** eine Tasse Tee *7 A*
cupboard ['kʌbəd] *der* (Küchen)Schrank *3 A*

D

dad [dæd] *der* Vater, *der* Vati *1 St 8*
dance [dɑːns] tanzen *5 I*
dangerous ['deɪndʒərəs] gefährlich *6 A*
date [deɪt] *das* Datum *10 T*
daughter ['dɔːtə] *die* Tochter *5 T*
day [deɪ] *der* Tag *6 T*: **one day** eines Tages *9 A*
December [dɪˈsembə] *der* Dezember *10 T*
desk [desk] *der* Schreibtisch *1 St 6*
difference ['dɪfrəns] *der* Unterschied *3 T*
different ['dɪfərənt] anders *11 D*
dinner ['dɪnə] *das* Abendessen *9 T*
do [duː] tun, machen *4 A*: **do the shopping** Einkäufe machen *8 A*
dog [dɒg] *der* Hund *3 A*
door [dɔː] *die* Tür *2 D*
double ['dʌbl] doppelt, hier: zweimal *10 B*
drama ['drɑːmə] Drama *11 B*
dress [dres] *das* Kleid *10 I*
drink [drɪŋk] *das* Getränk *9 A*

E

early ['ɜːlɪ] früh *3 D*
easy ['iːzɪ] einfach *6 T*
eat [iːt] essen, fressen *5 A*
eight [eɪt] acht *2 A*
eighty ['eɪtɪ] achtzig *7 A*
electrical shop [ɪˌlektrɪkl ˈʃɒp] *das* Elektrogeschäft *6 B*

elephant ['elɪfənt] *der* Elefant 5 A
eleven [ɪ'levn] elf 2 A
English ['ɪŋglɪʃ] *der* Engländer, *die* Engländerin; englisch(e, er, es) 1 I: **I'm not English** ich bin kein Engländer/keine Engländerin 1 St 3
English teacher ['ɪŋglɪʃ ˌtiːtʃə] *der* Englischlehrer, *die* Englischlehrerin 1 St 5
evening ['iːvnɪŋ] *der* Abend 4 I
every ['evrɪ] jede(r, s) 8 A
everybody ['evrɪbɒdɪ] jede(r, s) 8 D; alle 10 D
excuse me [ɪk'skjuːz miː] entschuldige/entschuldigen Sie, Verzeihung 10 A
exercise ['eksəsaɪz] *die* Übung 1 St 5
expensive [ɪk'spensɪv] teuer 6 A
eye [aɪ] *das* Auge 8 A

F

family ['fæməlɪ] *die* Familie 2 B
fantastic [fæn'tæstɪk] phantastisch 6 D
far [fɑː] fern 10 I
farm [fɑːm] *die* Farm, *der* Bauernhof 1 I
father ['fɑːðə] *der* Vater 2 T
favourite ['feɪvərɪt] liebstes, Lieblings- 11 A
February ['februərɪ] *der* Februar 10 T
ferry (*Mz: ferries*) ['ferɪ] *die* Fähre 11 A
festival ['festɪvəl] *das* Festival, *das* Fest 10 D
fetch [fetʃ] holen 4 D
few [fjuː]: **a few** ein paar 11 A
fifty ['fɪftɪ] fünfzig 7 A
film [fɪlm] *der* Film 1 I
find [faɪnd] finden 4 T
fine [faɪn]: **I'm fine** mir geht es gut/ausgezeichnet 1 St 4
finger ['fɪŋgə] *der* Finger 8 A
finish ['fɪnɪʃ] aufhören 11 T
fire ['faɪə] *das* Feuer 4 D
first [fɜːst] der/die/das erste 10 T
fish [fɪʃ] *der* Fisch 7 A
fisherman ['fɪʃəmən] *der* Fischer 3 D
fitness ['fɪtnɪs] Fitness 11 B
five [faɪv] fünf 2 A
flat [flæt] *die* Wohnung 9 A
flat [flæt] platt 3 A
flower ['flaʊə] *die* Blume 4 A

folk music ['fəʊk ˌmjuːzɪk] *die* Folkmusik 11 D
food [fuːd] *das* Futter, *die* Nahrung, *die* Lebensmittel 8 A
foot [fʊt] *der* Fuß 8 A
football ['fʊtbɔːl] Fußball 6 I
for [fɔː] für, nach 2 T
forget [fə'get] vergessen 5 A
forty ['fɔːtɪ] vierzig 7 A
four [fɔː] vier 2 A
fox [fɒks] *der* Fuchs 9 T
France ['frɑːns] Frankreich 7 A
free [friː] kostenlos 6 I
French [frentʃ] französisch; *der* Franzose, *die* Französin 7 A
Friday ['fraɪdɪ] *der* Freitag 5 A
friend [frend] *der* Freund, *die* Freundin 1 I
from [frɒm] von 4 T
fun [fʌn] *der* Spaß 6 I
funfair ['fʌnfeə] *der* Rummelplatz 10 D
funny ['fʌnɪ] komisch 8 A

G

Gaelic ['gælɪk] gälisch 11 A
game [geɪm] *das* Spiel 2 A
garden ['gɑːdn] *der* Garten 5 A
German ['dʒɜːmən] *der* Deutsche, *die* Deutsche; deutsch(e, er, es) 1 St 3
get [get] holen 3 A
get into [get ˈɪntə] hineinkommen 6 T
ghost [gəʊst] *der* Geist, *das* Gespenst 12 I
girl [gɜːl] *das* Mädchen 1 St 6
give [gɪv] geben 5 A
glad [glæd] froh 7 B
go [gəʊ] gehen 4 A: **go to bed** zu Bett gehen 5 D
go back to [gəʊ ˈbæk tə] zurückgehen zu 8 T
go down [gəʊ ˈdaʊn] hinuntergehen 10 A
go on to [gəʊ ˈɒn tə] weitergehen zu 8 T
good [gʊd] gut 1 St 2
good at ['gʊd ˌət] gut (in) 6 A
good morning! [gʊd ˈmɔːnɪŋ] guten Morgen! 1 St 2
good night! [gʊd ˈnaɪt] gute Nacht! 12 S 1
goodbye! [gʊd'baɪ] auf Wiedersehen! 2 I
goodness ['gʊdnɪs]: **my goodness!** ach du meine Güte!, ach du lieber Gott! 11 T

grandma ['grænmɑː] *umgangssprachlich:* die Großmutter, die Oma 10 D
grandmother ['grænmʌðə] *die* Großmutter 5 D
great [greɪt] großartig 2 A: **have a great time** sich amüsieren, großen Spaß haben 10 D
Greek [griːk] *der* Grieche, *die* Griechin; griechisch(e, er, es) 1 St 3
green [griːn] grün 10 I
greengrocer ['griːngrəʊsə] *der* Gemüsehändler 9 D: **go into the greengrocer's** in den Gemüseladen gehen 9 D
grey [greɪ] grau 10 I
group [gruːp] *die* Gruppe 6 D
guess [ges] raten 5 A

H

half [hɑːf]: **half past seven** halb acht 4 I
hall [hɔːl] *das* Herrenhaus, *das* Schloss 12 I
hamburger ['hæmbɜːgə] *der* Hamburger 11 D
hamster ['hæmstə] *der* Hamster 6 T
hand [hænd] *die* Hand 8 A
handbag ['hændbæg] *die* Handtasche 3 B
happen ['hæpən] passieren 12 S 4
happy ['hæpɪ] froh 4 T
hat [hæt] *der* Hut 10 I
have got [hæv 'gɒt] haben 2 A, 3 A
have got to [hæv 'gɒt tə] müssen 12 S 1
he [hiː] er 1 St 5: **he's** er ist 1 St 5
head [hed] *der* Kopf 8 A
hello! [hə'ləʊ] hallo!, guten Tag! 1 St 1
help [help] *die* Hilfe 3 D
help [help] helfen 4 A
her [hɜː] ihr(e) 1 St 7: **her** (*pers. Fürwort*) ihr, sie 7 A
here [hɪə] hier, da 1 St 8: **here you are** bitte schön 9 A
hey! [heɪ] he!, heda! 3 A
hill [hɪl] *der* Hügel 10 D
him [hɪm] ihn, ihm 7 A
his [hɪz] sein(e) 1 St 7
hobby (*Mz: hobbies*) ['hɒbɪ] *das* Hobby 7 D

home [həʊm]: **at home** zu Hause *2 A*
homework [ˈhəʊmwɜːk] *die* Hausaufgabe(n) *5 I*
honey [ˈhʌnɪ] *der* Honig *9 D*
hot [hɒt] heiß *4 B*
hotel [həʊˈtel] *das* Hotel *12 S 1*
house [haʊs] *das* Haus *1 St 8*
housewife [ˈhaʊswaɪf] *die* Hausfrau *11 A*
how? [hau] wie? *1 St 4*: **how are you?** wie geht es dir/Ihnen? *1 St 4*; **how many?** wie viele? *3 A*; **how much is …?** wie viel kostet …? *9 I*; **how old?** wie alt? *3 A*
hundred [ˈhʌndrɪd] hundert *2 A*: **a/one hundred** (ein)hundert *7 A*
hungry [ˈhʌŋgrɪ] hungrig *6 T*
hunter [ˈhʌntə] *der* Jäger *12 I*
hurt [hɜːt] weh tun *8 A*

I

I [aɪ] ich *1 St 1*: **I'm** ich bin *1 St 1*; **I am** ich bin *1 St 2*
idea [aɪˈdɪə] *die* Idee, *der* Einfall *6 A*
ill [ɪl] krank *4 A*
in [ɪn] in *2 I*: **in English** auf Englisch *1 St 6*
Indian [ˈɪndjən] *der* Inder, *die* Inderin; indisch *9 A*
interview [ˈɪntəvjuː] *das* Interview *11 D*
into [ˈɪntuː] in … (hinein) *5 A*
is [ɪz]: **he/she/it is** er/sie/es ist *1 St 5, 1 St 6*
it [ɪt] es, ihm *1 St 6*: **it's** es ist *1 St 6*
Italian [ɪˈtæljən] *der* Italiener, *die* Italienerin; italienisch(e, er, es) *1 St 3*

J

jacket [ˈdʒækɪt] *die* Jacke, *das* Jacket *10 I*
January [ˈdʒænjʊərɪ] *der* Januar *10 T*
jar [dʒɑː] *das* Glas *8 A*: **a jar of coffee** ein Glas Kaffee *8 A*
jeans *(Mz)* [dʒiːnz] *die* Jeans *10 I*
job [dʒɒb] *der* Job, *die* Stelle *11 A*
judo [ˈdʒuːdəʊ] Judo *6 I*: **judo is fun** Judo macht Spaß *6 A*

July [dʒuːˈlaɪ] *der* Juli *10 T*
June [dʒuːn] *der* Juni *10 D*

K

kilt [kɪlt] *der* Kilt, *der* Schottenrock *11 A*
knock [nɒk] *das* Klopfen *7 B*
know [nəʊ] kennen *11 A*: **I don't know** ich weiß nicht *9 B*

L

lady [ˈleɪdɪ] *die* Dame *7 A*
last [lɑːst] letzte(r, s) *11 A*
late [leɪt] (zu) spät *2 D*
lead [liːd] anführen *10 D*
learn [lɜːn] lernen *8 A*
left [left] links *10 A*: **on the left** auf der linken Seite *10 A*
leg [leg] *das* Bein *8 A*
let [let]: **let me …** lass mich … *6 T*; **let's go** lass(t) uns gehen, gehen wir *4 A*
letter [ˈletə] *der* Brief *7 D*; *der* Buchstabe *8 T*
like [laɪk] mögen, gern haben *7 A*: **I'd like** ich möchte bitte, ich hätte gern *8 A*; **like best** am liebsten mögen *11 A*
like this [laɪk ˈðɪs] so, auf diese Weise *5 T*
list [lɪst] *die* Liste *1 St 7*
listen to [ˈlɪsn tə] hören (auf), zuhören *1 St 4*
little [ˈlɪtl] klein *5 A*
live [lɪv] wohnen, leben *7 A*
London [ˈlʌndən] *Hauptstadt von Großbritannien 4 D*
look at [ˈlʊk ət] anschauen, ansehen *1 St 5*
look for [ˈlʊk fɔː] suchen nach *6 T*
Lord [lɔːd] Lord *(Titel) 12 I*
lot [ˈlɒt]: **a lot of** viel *6 A*
love [lʌv] lieben *9 A*
lunch [lʌntʃ] *das* Mittagessen *11 B*

M

madam [ˈmædəm] gnädige Frau *(Anrede für verheiratete Frauen) 12 S 1*
made in [ˈmeɪd ɪn] hergestellt in *7 A*
magazine [mægəˈziːn] *die* Zeitschrift *3 D*

magic [ˈmædʒɪk] magisch, Zauber- *7 T*
make [meɪk] machen *1 St 7*
man *(Mz: men)* [mæn, men] *der* Mann *3 A*
March [mɑːtʃ] *der* März *10 T*
match *(Mz: matches)* [mætʃ, ˈmætʃɪz] *das* Streichholz, *das* Zündholz *8 A*
match [mætʃ] kombinieren *9 D*
Maths [mæθs] Mathe(matik) *11 A*
matter [ˈmætə]: **what's the matter?** was ist los? *8 A*
May [meɪ] *der* Mai *10 T*
maybe [ˈmeɪbiː] vielleicht *8 A*
me [miː] mir, mich *4 A*
merry [ˈmerɪ] fröhlich *4 T*
message [ˈmesɪdʒ] *die* Botschaft *10 T*
midnight [ˈmɪdnaɪt] *die* Mitternacht *12 S 1*: **at midnight** um Mitternacht *12 S 1*
milk [mɪlk] *die* Milch *3 A*
Miss [mɪs] Fräulein *(Anrede) 1 St 2*
miss [mɪs] vermissen *11 A*; aussetzen *8 T*: **what's missing?** was fehlt? *2 A*
Monday [ˈmʌndɪ] Montag *8 A*
money [ˈmʌnɪ] *das* Geld *9 I*
monkey [ˈmʌŋkɪ] *der* Affe *3 A*
month [mʌnθ] *der* Monat *10 T*
more [mɔː] mehr *5 D*
morning [ˈmɔːnɪŋ] *der* Morgen *1 St 2*: **in the morning** am Morgen *3 D*
mother [ˈmʌðə] *die* Mutter *2 T*
mouth [maʊθ] *der* Mund *8 A*
move [muːv] ziehen *8 T*
Mr [ˈmɪstə] Herr *(Anrede) 1 St 2*
Mrs [ˈmɪsɪz] Frau *(Anrede) 1 St 2*
mum [mʌm] *die* Mutter, *die* Mutti *1 St 7*
music [ˈmjuːzɪk] *die* Musik *6 B*
must [mʌst] müssen *12 S 1*
my [maɪ] mein(e) *1 St 2*

N

name [neɪm] *der* Name *1 St 1*: **what's your name?** wie ist dein/Ihr Name?, wie heißt du?, wie heißen Sie? *1 St 1*; **my name is** mein Name ist, ich heiße *1 St 2*

near [nɪə] in der Nähe von, nahe bei *2 I*

need [niːd] brauchen *12 S 1*

neighbour ['neɪbə] *der* Nachbar, *die* Nachbarin *8 I*

never ['nevə] nie *11 T*

new [njuː] neu *1 I*

news *(Mz)* [njuːz] *die* Nachrichten *10 D*

newsagent ['njuːzeɪdʒənt] *der* Zeitungshändler *9 D*: **go into the newsagent's** zum Zeitungshändler gehen *9 D*

newspaper ['njuːspeɪpə] *die* Zeitung *4 T*

next [nekst] nächste(r, s) *10 A*

nice [naɪs] nett *1 St 5*

night [naɪt] *die* Nacht *12 S 1*: **'night!** *umgangssprachlich:* gute Nacht! *12 S 4*

nine [naɪn] neun *2 A*

ninety ['naɪntɪ] neunzig *7 A*

no [nəʊ] nein *1 St 3*; kein(e) *8 D*: **no more** keine ... mehr *8 D*

not [nɒt] nicht *1 St 3*

note [nəʊt] *die* Notiz *7 D*

November [nəʊ'vembə] *der* November *10 T*

now [naʊ] also, nun *1 St 6*; jetzt *1 St 1*

number ['nʌmbə] *die* Zahl, *die* Nummer *2 A*

O

October [ɒk'təʊbə] *der* Oktober *10 T*

of [ɒv, əv] von *2 I*

of course [əv 'kɔːs] selbstverständlich *9 D*

often ['ɒfn] oft *8 A*

oh! [əʊ] so!, ach! *1 St 3*: **oh dear!** ach du meine Güte!, oh je! *4 A*; **oh no!** ach du Schande! *4 A*

okay [əʊ'keɪ] in Ordnung *1 St 5*

old [əʊld] alt *2 I*

on [ɒn] auf *2 T*

one [wʌn] eins *2 A*

only ['əʊnlɪ] nur *6 A*

open ['əʊpən] öffnen *6 B*

open ['əʊpən] öffnen, aufmachen *6 T*

opinion [ə'pɪnjən] *die* Meinung *10 I*

or [ɔː] oder *1 T*

originally [ə'rɪdʒənəlɪ] ursprünglich *11 A*

other ['ʌðə] andere(r, s) *9 A*

our ['aʊə] unser(e, er, es) *2 A*

P

packet ['pækɪt] *die* Packung *8 A*: **a packet of tea** eine Packung Tee *8 A*

paper ['peɪpə] *das* Papier *2 T*: **a piece of paper** ein Blatt Papier, ein Zettel *2 T*

parade [pə'reɪd] *die* Parade, *der* Umzug *10 A*

pardon? ['pɑːdn] wie bitte? *9 D*

parents *(Mz)* ['peərənts] *die* Eltern *9 A*

part [pɑːt] *der* Teil *2 I*

partner ['pɑːtnə] *der* Partner, *die* Partnerin *1 St 7*

party ['pɑːtɪ] *die* Feier, *die* Party *5 D*

past [pɑːst] nach *4 I*

pen [pen] *der* Füllfederhalter, *der* Füller *1 St 6*

pencil ['pensl] *der* Bleistift *1 St 6*

penny, pence *(Mz)* (= p) ['penɪ, pens] *britische Münzeinheit 9 I*

people *(Mz)* ['piːpl] *die* Leute *1 St 5*

person ['pɜːsn] *die* Person *7 D*

pet [pet] *das* Haustier *3 A*

phone [fəʊn] anrufen, telefonieren *6 B*

phone call ['fəʊn kɔːl] *der* Telefonanruf, *das* Telefonat *5 A*

photo ['fəʊtəʊ] *das* Foto *2 T*

photograph ['fəʊtəgrɑːf] fotografieren *10 A*

photographer [fə'tɒgrəfə] *der* Fotograf *10 A*

Physical Education (= P.E.) [ˌfɪzɪkl ˌedjʊ'keɪʃn] Sport, Turnen *11 B*

picnic ['pɪknɪk] *das* Picknick *9 D*

picture ['pɪktʃə] *das* Bild *3 T*: **in the picture** auf dem Bild *3 T*

piece [piːs] *das* Stück *2 T*: **a piece of paper** ein Blatt Papier, ein Zettel *2 T*

pink [pɪŋk] pink *10 I*

pity ['pɪtɪ]: **what a pity!** wie schade! *6 A*

play [pleɪ] spielen *4 A*: **play cards** Karten spielen *5 I*

please [pliːz] bitte *1 St 6*

pocket ['pɒkɪt] *die* Tasche (*an Kleidungsstücken*) *3 T*

pop music ['pɒp ˌmjuːzɪk] *die* Popmusik *11 D*

port [pɔːt] *der* Hafen *2 I*

post office ['pəʊst ˌɒfɪs] *das* Postamt *10 B*

poster ['pəʊstə] *das* Poster, *das* Plakat *4 T*

postman ['pəʊstmən] *der* Postbote, *die* Postbotin; *der* Briefträger, *die* Briefträgerin *7 B*

pound (£) [paʊnd] *das* Pfund (*brit. Währung*) *9 I*

present ['preznt] *das* Geschenk *5 D*

problem ['prɒbləm] *das* Problem *3 I*

professor [prə'fesə] *der* Professor *1 T*

project ['prɒdʒekt] *das* Projekt *11 D*

pub [pʌb] *die* Kneipe, *das* Wirtshaus *11 A*

pullover ['pʊləʊvə] *der* Pullover *10 I*

pump [pʌmp] *die* (Luft)Pumpe *3 I*

pupil ['pjuːpl] *der* Schüler, *die* Schülerin *7 D*

put [pʊt] setzen, legen *4 A*

put on [pʊt ˈɒn] anziehen *10 D*

Q

quarter ['kwɔːtə]: **a quarter to nine** Viertel vor *neun 7 I*

question ['kwestʃən] *die* Frage *1 T*: **ask questions** Fragen stellen *11 A*

quick [kwɪk] schnell *6 T*

quiz [kwɪz] *das* Quiz *1 T*

R

read [riːd] lesen *3 D*

reader ['riːdə] *der* Leser, *die* Leserin *7 D*

really ['rɪəlɪ] eigentlich, wirklich *9 A*: **not really** eigentlich nicht *6 A*

red [red] rot *10 I*

Religious Education (= R.E.) [rɪˌlɪdʒəs edjʊ'keɪʃn] *der* Religionsunterricht *11 D*

report [rɪ'pɔːt] *der* Bericht *10 D*

revision [rɪ'vɪʒn] *die* Wiederholung *2 T*

rhyme [raɪm] *der* Reim, *der* Vers *2 D*

riddle ['rɪdl] *das* Rätsel *3 B*

right [raɪt] rechts *10 A:* **on the right** auf der rechten Seite *10 A*

right [raɪt] richtig *1 St 5*

rise up [raɪz ˈʌp] sich aufbäumen *3 D*

road [rəʊd] *die* Straße *10 A*

robot [ˈrɒbɒt] *der* Roboter *7 I*

room [ruːm, rʊm] *das* Zimmer *2 A*

rubber [ˈrʌbə] *der* Radiergummi *1 St 6*

run [rʌn] rennen *6 T*

run away [rʌn əˈweɪ] wegrennen *9 T*

S

sailor [ˈseɪlə] *der* Matrose, *der* Seemann *3 D*

Saturday [ˈsætədɪ] Sonnabend, Samstag *8 A*

say [seɪ] sagen *2 A:* **say hello** grüßen, einen Gruß ausrichten *12 S 4*

scene [siːn] *die* Szene *1 T*

school [skuːl] *die* Schule *7 D*

school bag [ˈskuːl bæg] *die* Schultasche, -mappe *1 St 6*

Science [ˈsaɪəns] Naturwissenschaften *11 D*

Scotland [ˈskɒtlənd] Schottland *11 I*

Scots [skɒts] *die* Schotten *11 A*

Scottish [ˈskɒtɪʃ] *der* Schotte, *die* Schottin; schottisch(e, er, es) *1 St 3*

scream [skriːm] schreien, kreischen *10 D*

sea [siː] *das* Meer *8 T*

season [ˈsiːzn] *die* Jahreszeit *10 T*

second [ˈsekənd] der/die/das zweite *10 T*

secret [ˈsiːkrɪt] geheim *11 T*

see [siː] sehen *6 T:* **I see** (ich) verstehe, ah ja *12 S 1*

sell [sel] verkaufen *8 T*

sentence [ˈsentəns] *der* Satz *9 D*

September [sepˈtembə] *der* September *10 T*

seven [ˈsevn] sieben *2 A*

seventy [ˈsevntɪ] siebzig *7 A*

she [ʃiː] sie *1 St 5:* **she's** sie ist *1 St 5*

ship [ʃɪp] *das* Schiff *3 D*

shirt [ʃɜːt] *das* Hemd *10 I*

shoe [ʃuː] *der* Schuh *10 I*

shop [ʃɒp] *der* Laden, *das* Geschäft *1 I*

shop [ʃɒp] einkaufen *4 A*

shopping day [ˈʃɒpɪŋ deɪ] *der* Einkaufstag *8 A*

shopping list [ˈʃɒpɪŋ lɪst] *die* Einkaufsliste *8 A*

shut up [ʃʌt ˈʌp] ruhig sein, den Mund halten *7 A*

silly [ˈsɪlɪ] dumm, albern *10 A*

sing [sɪŋ] singen *1 St 4*

sir [sɜː] mein Herr *(Anrede) 9 D*

sister [ˈsɪstə] *die* Schwester *1 St 4*

sit down [sɪt ˈdaʊn] sich (hin)setzen *1 St 6*

six [sɪks] sechs *2 A*

sixty [ˈsɪkstɪ] sechzig *7 A*

skirt [skɜːt] *der* Rock *10 I*

sleep [sliːp] schlafen *5 I*

small [smɔːl] klein *1 St 7*

smart [smɑːt] schick *10 I*

so [səʊ] also, daher *9 T;* (al)so *12 S 1*

sock [sɒk] *die* Socke *10 I*

some [sʌm] etwas *3 D*

sometimes [ˈsʌmtaɪmz] manchmal *8 A*

son [sʌn] *der* Sohn *5 T*

song [sɒŋ] *das* Lied *1 St 4*

sorry! [ˈsɒrɪ] Entschuldigung!, Verzeihung! *1 St 8:* **I'm sorry** es tut mir leid, Verzeihung *12 S 4*

sound [saʊnd] *der* Laut, *der* Klang *1 I*

speak [spiːk] sprechen *7 A*

spell [spel] buchstabieren *10 B*

sport [spɔːt] *der* Sport *1 I*

spring [sprɪŋ] *der* Frühling *9 T*

square [skweə] *das* Quadrat *7 T*

squash [skwɒʃ] Squash *6 I*

stall [stɔːl] *die* Bude *10 D*

stand up [stænd ˈʌp] aufstehen *1 St 6*

start [stɑːt] anfangen *1 I*

station [steɪʃn] *der* Bahnhof *10 B*

stay [steɪ] bleiben *12 S 1*

step [step] *der* Schritt *1 St 1*

stereo [ˈsteriəʊ] *die* Stereoanlage *2 A*

stick [stɪk] anheften, kleben *2 T*

stop [stɒp] aufhören *1 I*

story [ˈstɔːrɪ] *die* Geschichte *6 T*

street [striːt] *die* Straße *5 A:* **in the street** auf der Straße *5 A*

subject [ˈsʌbdʒɪkt] *das* Schulfach *11 A*

sugar [ˈʃʊɡə] *der* Zucker *3 A:* **a bag og sugar** eine Tüte Zucker *8 A*

summer [ˈsʌmə] *der* Sommer *6 T*

Sunday [ˈsʌndɪ] Sonntag *8 A*

super [ˈsuːpə] super *7 A*

supermarket [ˈsuːpəmɑːkɪt] *der* Supermarkt *9 D*

survey [ˈsɜːveɪ] *die* Umfrage *6 D*

sweets *(Mz)* [swiːts] *die* Süßigkeiten *3 D*

swimming [ˈswɪmɪŋ] *das* Schwimmen *6 A*

swimming pool [ˈswɪmɪŋ puːl] *das* Schwimmbad *6 Aq*

T

T-shirt [ˈtiːʃɜːt] *das* T-Shirt *10 I*

table [ˈteɪbl] *der* Tisch *1 St 6*

take [teɪk] nehmen *2 T;* bringen *4 A:* **take a photo** [teɪk ə ˈfəʊtəʊ] ein Foto machen *12 S 1*

talk [tɔːk] *das* Gespräch *1 St 10*

talk about [ˈtɔːk əˌbaʊt] sprechen über/von *1 St 5*

talk to [ˈtɔːk tə] reden mit *4 A*

task [tɑːsk] *die* Aufgabe *1 T*

tea [tiː] *der* Tee *3 A:* **a cup of tea** eine Tasse Tee *7 A;* **a packet of tea** eine Packung Tee *8 A*

teacher [ˈtiːtʃə] *der* Lehrer, *die* Lehrerin *1 St 5*

team [tiːm] *die* Mannschaft, *das* Team *1 I*

teatime [ˈtiːtaɪm] *die* Teestunde *3 A*

teddy bear [ˈtedɪ beə] *der* Teddybär *9 D*

telephone [ˈtelɪfəʊn] *das* Telefon *1 T*

telephone number [ˈtelɪfəʊn ˌnʌmbə] *die* Telefonnummer *2 B*

television [ˈtelɪvɪʒn] *der* Fernseher *2 A*

tell about [ˈtel əˌbaʊt] erzählen von *7 D*

ten [ten] zehn *2 A*

tennis [ˈtenɪs] Tennis *6 I*

terrible [ˈterəbl] schrecklich, furchtbar *12 S 5*

test [test] prüfen, testen *1 I*

text [tekst] *der* Text *5 D*

thank you [ˈθæŋk juː] danke, danke schön *4 A*

thanks [θæŋks] danke 1 St 4
that [ðæt] der, die, das (da); jene(r, s) 1 St 5: **that's** [ðæts] das ist *1 St 5*
that's six pounds [ðæts 'sɪks 'paʊndz] das kostet/macht sechs Pfund 9 I
the [ðə] der, die, das 1 St 5
their [ðeə] ihr(e) 3 I
them [ðem] ihnen, sie 5 A
then [ðen] dann 5 A
there [ðeə]: **there is** es gibt, da ist 6 A; **there are** es gibt, da sind 6 A; **there's** [ðeəz] es gibt, da ist 6 A
they [ðeɪ] sie (*Mz*) 1 St 10: **they're** ['ðeə] sie sind 1 St 10
thing [θɪŋ] *das* Ding, *die* Sache 3 D: **things are fine** alles läuft gut 9 A
think [θɪŋk] nachdenken, überlegen 6 T
third [θɜːd] der/die/das dritte *10 T*
thirteen [θɜː'tiːn] dreizehn 7 A
thirty ['θɜːtɪ] dreißig 7 A
this [ðɪs] diese(r, s); das 1 St 4
three [θriː] drei 2 A
Thursday ['θɜːzdɪ] Donnerstag 8 A: **on Thursdays** donnerstags 8 A
till [tɪl] bis *3 D*
time [taɪm] *die* Zeit 2 T, 4 I: **what's the time?** wie viel Uhr ist es? 4 I; **what time?** um wie viel Uhr?, wann? *5 A*
timetable ['taɪmteɪbl] *der* Stundenplan *11 D*
tin [tɪn] *die* Büchse, *die* Dose 3 D
tired ['taɪəd] müde 6 T
to [tʊ] zu(m) 4 A; vor 7 I
today [tə'deɪ] heute *1 St 4*, 8 A
together [tə'geðə] miteinander, zusammen 4 D
too [tuː] auch 2 T
tourist ['tʊərɪst] *der* Tourist 12 S 1
town [taʊn] *die* Stadt 2 I
toy [tɔɪ] *das* Spielzeug 7 A
traditional [trə'dɪʃənəl] traditionell, überliefert 4 D
traffic lights (*Mz*) ['træfɪk laɪts] *die* Ampel *10 A*
tree [triː] *der* Baum *4 T*
trousers (*Mz*) ['traʊzəz] *die* Hose 10 I
Tuesday ['tjuːzdɪ] Dienstag 8 A

Turkish ['tɜːkɪʃ] *der* Türke, *die* Türkin; türkisch(e, er, es) 1 St 3
turn [tɜːn] abbiegen 10 A
turn [tɜːn] *die* Runde *8 T*: **it's your turn** du bist an der Reihe 2 D
twelve [twelv] zwölf 2 A
twenty ['twentɪ] zwanzig 7 A
twenty-one [twentɪ'wʌn] einundzwanzig 7 A
two [tuː] zwei 2 A
tyre ['taɪə] *der* Reifen *3 A*: **flat tyre** *die* Reifenpanne, *der* Platten *3 A*

U

uncle ['ʌŋkl] *der* Onkel 2 T
under ['ʌndə] unter 6 T
uniform ['juːnɪfɔːm] *die* Uniform *10 I*
unit ['juːnɪt] *die* Lektion *1 I*
up [ʌp] oben *9 T*
us [ʌs] uns 6 A
usually ['juːʒʊəlɪ] gewöhnlich, meistens 11 T

V

vegetables (*Mz*) ['vedʒtəblz] *das* Gemüse 4 A
very ['verɪ] sehr 1 St 7
video ['vɪdɪəʊ] *das* Video(gerät) 2 A
violet ['vaɪələt] violett *10 I*
visit ['vɪzɪt] besuchen 5 D
volleyball ['vɒlɪbɔːl] Volleyball 6 I

W

wait [weɪt] warten *12 S 1*
walk [wɔːk] gehen 7 A
want [wɒnt] wollen, wünschen 9 A
warm [wɔːm] warm *4 B*
wash [wɒʃ] waschen 4 A
watch TV (= *television*) [wɒtʃ tiː'viː] fernsehen 5 A
water ['wɔːtə] *das* Wasser *4 D*
way [weɪ] *der* Weg 10 A
we [wiː] wir 1 St 9: **we shall** wir sollen *3 D*; **we're** wir sind 1 St 9
wear [weə] (*Kleidung*) tragen, anhaben 10 I
Wednesday ['wenzdɪ] Mittwoch 8 A

week [wiːk] *die* Woche *8 A*
welcome to ['welkəm tə] willkommen in/im *6 D*
well [wel] also *6 A*
what? [wɒt] was? 1 St 1: **what's** was ist? 1 St 1
what about ...? ['wɒt ə,baʊt] was ist mit ...?, wie steht es mit ...? 1 St 8
when? [wen] wann? 11 A; wenn *12 S 4*
where? [weə] wo? 4 A; wohin *6 A*: **where's?** wo ist? *4 A*
white [waɪt] weiß 10 I
who? [huː] wer? 1 St 5: **who's?** wer ist? 1 St 5
whose? [huːz] wessen? *8 A*
window ['wɪndəʊ] *das* Fenster 1 St 6
winner ['wɪnə] *der* Gewinner, *die* Gewinnerin; *der* Sieger, *die* Siegerin *8 T*
winter ['wɪntə] *der* Winter *10 T*
wish [wɪʃ] wünschen *4 T*
with [wɪð] mit 4 A
woman (*Mz:* **women**) ['wʊmən, 'wɪmɪn] *die* Frau 4 A
wonderful ['wʌndəfʊl] wunderbar *6 T*
wood [wʊd] *der* Wald *9 D*
word [wɜːd] *das* Wort 1 I
work [wɜːk] arbeiten 7 I
worm [wɜːm] *der* Wurm *3 D*
write about ['raɪt ə,baʊt] schreiben über 2 T
wrong [rɒŋ] falsch 1 St 5

Y

year [jɪə] *das* Jahr *4 T*
yellow ['jeləʊ] gelb 10 I
yes [jes] ja 1 St 2
you [juː] du, Sie, ihr 1 St 2: **you're** [jʊə] du bist 1 St 7; **you** (*pers. Fürwort*) dir, dich / ihnen, sie / Ihnen, Sie 1 St 9
your [jɔː] dein(e), Ihr(e) 1 St 1

Numbers

1	one	[wʌn]	1st	the **first**	[ðə 'fɜːst]
2	two	[tuː]	2nd	the **second**	[ðə 'sekənd]
3	three	[θriː]	3rd	the **third**	[ðə 'θɜːd]
4	four	[fɔː]	4th	the fourth	[ðə 'fɔːθ]
5	five	[faɪv]	5th	the **fifth**	[ðə 'fɪfθ]
6	six	[sɪks]	6th	the sixth	[ðə 'sɪksθ]
7	seven	[sevn]	7th	the seventh	[ðə 'sevnθ]
8	eight	[eɪt]	8th	the **eighth**	[ðiː 'eɪtθ]
9	nine	[naɪn]	9th	the **ninth**	[ðə 'naɪnθ]
10	ten	[ten]	10th	the tenth	[ðə 'tenθ]
11	eleven	[ɪ'levn]	11th	the eleventh	[ðiː ɪ'levnθ]
12	twelve	[twelv]	12th	the **twelfth**	[ðə 'twelfθ]
13	thirteen	[ˌθɜː'tiːn]	13th	the thirteenth	[ðə ˌθɜː'tiːnθ]
14	fourteen	[ˌfɔː'tiːn]	14th	the fourteenth	[ðə ˌfɔː'tiːnθ]
15	fifteen	[ˌfɪf'tiːn]	15th	the fifteenth	[ðə ˌfɪf'tiːnθ]
16	sixteen	[ˌsɪks'tiːn]	16th	the sixteenth	[ðə ˌsɪks'tiːnθ]
17	seventeen	[ˌsevn'tiːn]	17th	the seventeenth	[ðə ˌsevn'tiːnθ]
18	eighteen	[ˌeɪ'tiːn]	18th	the eighteenth	[ðiː ˌeɪ'tiːnθ]
19	nineteen	[ˌnaɪn'tiːn]	19th	the nineteenth	[ðə ˌnaɪn'tiːnθ]
20	twenty	['tewntɪ]	20th	the **twentieth**	[ðə 'twentɪəθ]
21	twenty-one	[ˌtwentɪ'wʌn]	21st	the twenty-first	[ðə ˌtwentɪ'fɜːst]
30	thirty	['θɜːtɪ]	22nd	the twenty-second	[ðə ˌtwentɪ'sekənd]
40	forty	['fɔːtɪ]	23rd	the twenty-third	[ðə ˌtwentɪ'θɜːd]
50	fifty	['fɪftɪ]	24th	the twenty-fourth	[ðə ˌtwentɪ'fɔːθ]
60	sixty	['sɪkstɪ]	25th	the twenty-fifth	[ðə ˌtwentɪ'fɪfθ]
70	seventy	['sevntɪ]	26th	the twenty-sixth	[ðə ˌtwentɪ'sɪksθ]
80	eighty	['eɪtɪ]	27th	the twenty-seventh	[ðə ˌtwentɪ'sevnθ]
90	ninety	['naɪntɪ]	28th	the twenty-eighth	[ðə ˌtwentɪ'eɪtθ]
100	a hundred	[ə 'hʌndrəd]	29th	the twenty-ninth	[ðə ˌtwentɪ'naɪnθ]
	one hundred	[ˌwʌn 'hʌndrəd]	30th	the **thirtieth**	[ðə 'θɜːtɪəθ]

Letters

a	[eɪ]	d	[diː]	g	[dʒiː]	j	[dʒeɪ]	m	[em]	p	[piː]	s	[es]
b	[biː]	e	[iː]	h	[eɪtʃ]	k	[keɪ]	n	[en]	q	[kjuː]	t	[tiː]
c	[siː]	f	[ef]	i	[aɪ]	l	[el]	o	[əʊ]	r	[ɑː]	u	[juː]

v	[viː]	y	[waɪ]
w	['dʌbljuː]	z	[zed]
x	[eks]		

Sounds

Vowels/Vokale/Selbstlaute

- [ɪ] it, six, big
- [e] pet, tell, friend
- [æ] bad, thanks, man
- [ʌ] cup, come, number
- [ɒ] what, on, dog
- [ʊ] put, look, good
- [ə] a sailor, sister, German

- [iː] tea, street, please
- [ɑː] car, father, garden
- [ɔː] door, four, small
- [uː] two, food, judo
- [ɜː] girl, German, Turkish

- [eɪ] name, they, play
- [aɪ] nice, fine, five
- [ɔɪ] boy, toy
- [aʊ] now, house, about
- [əʊ] no, know, hello
- [ɪə] here, dear, near
- [eə] chair, their, there
- [ʊə] tourist

Consonants/Konsonanten/Mitlaute

- [p] pencil, pump
- [b] baby, table, club
- [t] tea, street
- [d] door, window, food
- [k] car, book
- [g] girl, again, bag

- [f] fine, photo, often
- [v] very, have, five
- [θ] thanks, month
- [ð] this, mother, with
- [s] six, cassettes
- [z] easy, does, his
- [ʃ] she, Scottish
- [ʒ] television
- [tʃ] chair, teacher, church
- [dʒ] German, George
- [m] milk, summer, time
- [n] no, know, woman
- [ŋ] sing, uncle, monkey
- [l] letter, yellow, little
- [j] yes, new, unit
- [w] we, what, twelve, question

- [r] read, dress, very
- [h] here, who, bighead

- [ː] der vorangehende Laut ist lang [tuː]
- ['] Hauptbetonung: die folgende Silbe ist betont [ɪ'levn]
- [ˌ] Nebenbetonung: die folgende Silbe ist betont, aber schwächer als beim Hauptton [ˌθɜː'tiːn]
- [‿] die beiden Laute werden verbunden [ˌpɒt‿'ɒn]

Acknowledgements

We are grateful to the following for permission to reproduce/use copyright material:

Texts and songs:

Prof. Dr. Gerngroß, Prof. Dr. H. Puchta, Graz, Univ. Doz. Dr. M. Schratz, Innsbruck for "The box of nuts": page 62 and for "The clever crow": page 89

Longman Group UK Ltd., Harlow for "Good Morning" from *Jigsaw Songs* by Trevor Jones and Brian Abbs: page 4 and for the "ABC song" from *Welcome to English* by Martin Bates: page 95

Illustrations:

Jürgen Bartz, München: pages IV, XII, 57 (No 2), 95 (top left), 128 (left)

Erhard Dietl, Ottobrunn: pages 44 (bottom left), 89

Dover Publications, Inc., New York: page 54, 57 (top left: Nos 1, 3, 4)) from *Handbook of Pictorial Symbols*

Barbara Köhler, München: pages 30, 105

Jörg Plannerer, München: pages III (top), 1 (top), 3 (top right), 5 (middle right, bottom), 7, 8, 9 (middle right, bottom right) 10 (top, middle), 12 (top right, left), 13 (bottom), 14, 16, 17, 21, 23, 28, 29, 34 (middle), 38 (middle, bottom), 39 (top), 40 (right), 42 (left), 43 (bottom), 44 (top, middle), 48, 49, 50, 53 (Nos 1-5), 58, 62, 67, 70, 71 (top, bottom right), 76, 78, 80, 81, 84 (bottom), 86, 87, 88, 94, 95 (top right), 96, 100, 107, 109, 111, 117 (Nos 1, 13; ghost; bottom left), 119 (bottom right), 120, 124, 128 (bottom), 130, 132

Peter Stevenson, Linden Artists Ltd, London: pages III (bottom), V-XI, 1 (bottom), 2, 3 (top left), 4, 5 (top, middle left), 6, 9 (top, middle left, bottom left), 10 (bottom), 11, 12 (bottom right), 13 (top) 15, 19, 22 (right), 24, 25 (bottom), 26, 27, 32 (top, bottom right), 33, 35, 36, 37, 40 (bottom left), 42 (right), 43 (top), 46 (bottom), 47, 51, 52, 56, 59, 61, 63-66, 68, 71 (bottom left), 73-75, 77 (top left), 83, 84 (top), 85, 90-92, 95 (middle right), 97, 99, 103, 110, 112, 114, 115, 117 (Nos 12,18,19;top right), 118 (middle, bottom left), 119 (left)

David Vaughan, München: pages 20, 22 (top left), 25 (top), 32 (bottom left), 34 (top, bottom), 38 (top), 39 (bottom), 45 (top), 46 (top), 53 (bottom), 57 (bottom), 77 (bottom), 79, 82, 98, 116, 117 (middle right), 118 (top right/left, bottom right)

Photographs:

Beate Andler-Teufel, München: page 109 (left)

Barnaby's Picture Library, London: pages 72 (No 3: Bill Coward), 79, 102 (No 4)

Jürgen Bartz, München: page 72 (Nos 2, 7)

Dr. Siegfried Birle, München: pages XII (top and middle left), 72 (No 6)

Britain on View, London: pages 18 (No 2), 72 (No 5), 102 (No 3)

Dick Castledine, Harlow: page 109 (right)

COI, Central Office of Information, London: page 18 (Nos 1, 6)

dpa-Bilderdienst, Frankfurt: page XII (bottom right)

Laurence Harger, Nürnberg: page 18 (Nos 3, 4, 5)

IFA-Bilderteam GmbH, München-Taufkirchen: cover, pages I (Bürgel), 72 (No 1: A. Prenzel; No 4: Löhr)

Peter Illmeier, Graz: page 69

Thomas Müller, Darmstadt: page 61 (left)

Nusser-Verlag, München: page 102 (No 1)

W. Rudolph Dia-Archiv, München: page 102 (No 2; middle)

Marion Schweitzer Photo-Agentur/Bildarchiv: page XII (bottom left)

Visual Publications, London: page 61 (right)

The traditional song "London's burning" on page 42 was taken from *Songs and Rhymes for the Teaching of English* by Julian Dakin, Longman Group UK Ltd., Harlow.